Structure & Speaking Practice
Barcelona

NATIONAL GEOGRAPHIC
L E A R N I N G

Australia • Brazil • Mexico • Singapore • United Kingdom • United States

National Geographic Learning,
a Cengage Company

Structure & Speaking Practice, Barcelona

Becky Tarver Chase and Christien Lee

Publisher: Sherrise Roehr

Executive Editor: Laura LeDréan

Managing Editor: Jennifer Monaghan

Digital Implementation Manager,
Irene Boixareu

Senior Media Researcher: Leila Hishmeh

Director of Global Marketing: Ian Martin

Regional Sales and National Account
Manager: Andrew O'Shea

Content Project Manager: Ruth Moore

Senior Designer: Lisa Trager

Manufacturing Planner: Mary Beth
Hennebury

Composition: Lumina Datamatics

Student Edition: Structure & Speaking Practice, Barcelona
ISBN-13: 978-0-357-13800-7

National Geographic Learning
20 Channel Center Street
Boston, MA 02210
USA

Locate your local office at **international.cengage.com/region**

Visit National Geographic Learning online at **ELTNGL.com**
Visit our corporate website at **www.cengage.com**

Printed in China

Print Number: 02   Print Year: 2019

Photo credits

Scope and Sequence

Speaking & Presentation	Vocabulary	Grammar & Pronunciation	Critical Thinking
• Using Numbers and Statistics • Looking Up While Speaking **Lesson Task** Discussing Small Businesses **Final Task** Presenting a Socially Responsible Business	Suffix -ive	• Indirect Questions • Pronouncing Large Numbers	**Focus** Personalizing Evaluating, Analyzing, Synthesizing, Interpreting Statistics, Organizing Ideas
• Using Phrases to Signal Reasons • Practicing and Timing Your Presentation **Lesson Task** Discussing Claims about Public Health **Final Task** A Presentation on Medicine and Health	Word Families	• Adverb Clauses of Reason and Purpose • Linking Vowel Sounds with /y/ and /w/	**Focus** Evaluating Claims Making Inferences, Evaluating, Personalizing, Applying, Brainstorming, Organizing Ideas
• Defending an Opinion • Interacting with the Audience **Lesson Task** Presenting Survey Results **Final Task** Presenting Research	Identifying Latin Prefixes and Suffixes	• *Used to* and *Would* • Using Punctuation Marks	**Focus** Making Judgments Analyzing, Personalizing, Synthesizing, Categorizing, Making Inferences, Evaluating, Applying, Judging, Organizing Ideas

Independent Student Handbook, p. 61   Vocabulary Index, p. 76

MAKING A LIVING, MAKING A DIFFERENCE

games
photos
videos
television
favorites
news
profile

**National Geographic Explorer
Tan Le wears a special headset
that reads brainwaves, making
it possible to control virtual and
physical objects with thoughts.**

ACADEMIC SKILLS

LISTENING Listening for Similarities and Contrasts
Using Abbreviations

SPEAKING Using Numbers and Statistics
Indirect Questions

CRITICAL THINKING Personalizing

THINK AND DISCUSS

1 How can Tan Le's invention make a difference in
people's lives?

2 Think about the unit title. How can a person make a
difference in the lives of others while making a living?

Look at the photos and read the information. Then discuss the questions.

1. How do you think each person feels about his or her job?
2. How are these people making a difference through their work? In other words, how are they helping others?
3. What type of work is most interesting to you? Why?

WAYS OF WORKING

Three entrepreneurs work in a start-up company in Amman, Jordan.

A factory worker assembles electronic switches in Shanghai, China.

A bakery owner stands in front of his shop in Bodrum, Turkey.

A nurse checks a boy before surgery in Bharatpur, Nepal.

A Vocabulary

A Mark the words you already know. Then use a dictionary to look up the others.

conventional (adj) cooperate (v) diverse (adj) models (n) profits (n)

B 🎧 **Track 1** Fill in each blank with a word from exercise A. Then listen and check your answers.

COOPERATIVES

Cooperatives, or co-ops, are different from corporations or other

_____ business _____. The main difference is
1   2

that the employees are also the owners of the cooperative. They agree to

_____ by selling their products or services together rather than
3

separately. If the co-op makes money, the members share the _____.
4

This allows all co-op members to earn a good living.

Cooperative businesses are quite _____. They provide every
5

imaginable kind of goods and services and can range from quite large to very

small. For example, in Boston, computer experts decided to work for themselves

and formed TechCollective. At TechCollective, customers can simply walk in and

have their computer problems solved by the same people who own the business.

C With a partner, discuss the questions below.

1. According to the article, what are the benefits of cooperatives to members?
2. Do you think a cooperative would earn higher or lower profits than a conventional business? Why?
3. As a customer, would you like to get products or services from a co-op? Why or why not?

D Mark the words you already know. Then use a dictionary to look up the others.

assess (v) effective (adj) entrepreneurs (n) generate (v) poverty (n)

E 🎧 **Track 2** Fill in each blank with a word from exercise D. Then listen and check your answers.

MEANING FROM
CONTEXT

PERUVIAN WEAVERS:
A PROFITABLE ARTISAN¹ COOPERATIVE

In the Andes Mountains of Peru, people in the village of Chinchero were living in _____ during much of the 20th century. Their agricultural products—potatoes, barley, and sheep—were bringing in very little income. In 1996, the women of Chinchero became _____ and started the Chinchero Weaving Cooperative. They began selling their traditional handmade fabrics to tourists. Now, the women _____ more income for their work, and their earnings stay within the community. Starting a co-op was a(n) _____ way for villagers in Chinchero to bring in more money. However, before deciding to start a cooperative, owners of small, home-based businesses need to _____ their situation carefully.

A weaver in the Chinchero community, Sacred Valley of the Incas, Peru

¹**artisan** (n): a person who is skilled at making something by hand

F Work in a small group. Discuss these questions.

CRITICAL THINKING: EVALUATING

1. How did forming the cooperative help families generate more income in Chinchero?
2. Why is it important to have diverse kinds of businesses in a community; for example, large department stores, small family-owned businesses, and entrepreneurs?

VOCABULARY SKILL Suffix –ive

We can add the suffix –ive to some verbs to form adjectives. The adjective form means tending to or having the quality of. Notice the spelling changes.

addict → addict**ive**	effect → effect**ive**	compete → competit**ive**
create → creat**ive**	decide → decis**ive**	persuade → persuas**ive**

G With a partner, change each verb into an adjective with the *-ive* suffix. Then write a sentence with each adjective in your notebook. Use a dictionary as needed.

cooperate _____   interact _____   attract _____

communicate _____   express _____   protect _____

Listening A Talk about a Cooperative Business

A cobra at the Irula Snake-Catchers' Cooperative, Chennai, India

BEFORE LISTENING

CRITICAL THINKING: ANALYZING

A 🎧 **Track 3** Read and listen to the information. Then discuss the questions with a partner.

> **SNAKE HUNTERS FIND CURE FOR JOBLESSNESS**
>
> Most people run away when they see a poisonous snake—but not the Irulas of India. For generations, the Irulas made their living by catching wild snakes, including deadly poisonous cobras. In the past, the snakes' skins were sold and made into luxury goods such as handbags and boots. But that changed in 1972, when the Indian Parliament adopted the Wildlife Protection Act, making the Irulas' main income source suddenly illegal.

1. Why do you think the 1972 law was passed?
2. What other situations might force people to change the way they make a living?

NOTE-TAKING SKILL Using Abbreviations

You can take notes more quickly by using abbreviations, or shortened forms of words. An abbreviation can be just part of a word, or it might be only a few letters. Here are some common abbreviations, but any system that makes sense to you will help make your note taking faster.

corp. = corporation	*info. = information*	*org. = organization*	*w/ = with*
hosp. = hospital	*mktg. = marketing*	*vs. = versus*	*w/o = without*

WHILE LISTENING

B 🎧 Track 4 ▶ 1.1 Read the notes outlining the main ideas. Then listen and complete the notes using abbreviations.

Spkr: Marsha Nolan, _____ of Worldwide Co-op
                               1

Topic today: _____ about co-op in India
                     2

Irula tribe: - Pre-1972, caught snakes such as _____ cobra; sold skins for $
                                            3

        (but lived in _____)
                         4

        - After 1972, became _____ (started a co-op); now milk snakes
                                     5

        for venom (used for anti-venom, cures snakebites)

Benefits: - Snakes not killed; 1000s of _____ lives saved; Irulas earn more
                                           6

C 🎧 Track 4 Listen again and choose the correct answer.

LISTENING FOR DETAILS

1. According to the speaker, what does Worldwide Co-op offer to cooperatives?
   a. bank loans   b. online information   c. health insurance

2. Each year, how many people in India die from snakebites?
   a. 26,000   b. 36,000   c. 46,000

3. How many members does the Irula co-op have?
   a. 200   b. 300   c. 400

4. What kind of organizations do the people in the audience belong to?
   a. wildlife organizations   b. medical organizations   c. youth organizations

AFTER LISTENING

D In a small group, discuss the three co-ops. How has each co-op directly benefited its members? What other positive effects do you think each co-op might have on the community or on the world? Compare your notes with another group.

CRITICAL THINKING: SYNTHESIZING

	Benefits to Members	Other Positive Effects
TechCollective		
Chinchero Weaving Cooperative		
Irula Snake-Catchers' Cooperative		

MAKING A LIVING, MAKING A DIFFERENCE   **7**

A Speaking

Numbers and statistics will support your ideas and make them more convincing.

Less convincing: *There are many deaths from snakebites in India each year, so a lot of anti-venom is needed.*

More convincing: *With **approximately 46,000** deaths from snakebites in India each year, there is a huge demand for anti-venom.*

In speaking, there may be more than one way to express a number.

2,700   *Twenty-seven hundred / Two thousand seven hundred*

A Work with a partner. Practice saying the numbers.

1. 250   two fifty / two hundred and fifty

2. 4,900   forty-nine hundred / four thousand nine hundred

3. 728,000   seven hundred and twenty-eight thousand

4. 1,000,000   one million

5. 1.5 million   one point five million

6. 7,000,000,000   seven billion

B 🎧 **Track 5** Work with a partner. In your notebook, write out how you would say each number. Then listen and check your answers.

1. 50,000   3. 9,600   5. 8,000,000,000

2. 3,200,000   4. 740,000   6. 1,297,300

C 🎧 **Track 6** With a partner, discuss where you think each number below should go in the paragraph. Then listen and check your answers.

7.4   18   60   85   2,500

Kudzu, originally brought to the United States from Japan in 1876, is an invasive plant species. During the 1930s, the U.S. government provided farmers with _____ million kudzu seedlings to hold dry soil in place. That may have been a mistake because kudzu can grow very quickly—up to _____ feet, or _____ meters, in one growing season. It can cover as many as _____ acres of land each year. Currently, kudzu covers around _____ million acres of land in the United States.

D In a small group, read about an entrepreneur who is making a profit from kudzu. Then discuss the questions below.

NANCY BASKET'S KUDZU MAGIC

Nancy Basket is a Native American artist who runs a small business, Kudzu Kabin Designs, from her home in South Carolina, in the United States. She is one of a few people who sees the benefits of the vine that most Americans hate. "It's very invasive. It grows 12 inches (30 centimeters) every single day, and people haven't been able to use it. But I use it for everything, and people can buy it (from me) in a form that's guaranteed to never grow again," Basket said.

In addition to her baskets, she sells lamp shades made from kudzu vines, and cards and posters made from kudzu paper. Even her artist's studio is made out of kudzu bales[1]—the only such structure of its kind. From an invasive and destructive plant, Basket has created a successful business.

[1]**bales** (n): large cubes of material such as hay, paper, or kudzu tied together tightly

1. Would you be interested in buying Basket's products? If so, which ones?
2. How is her business similar to and different from the Irula Snake-Catchers' Cooperative?
3. Do you think that kudzu entrepreneurs can effectively reduce the amount of kudzu in the United States? Why or why not?
4. Making a product is only part of what Basket does. Discuss in what ways each activity listed below is important to a small business owner. What other responsibilities does an owner have?

   - marketing and advertising a product
   - maintaining a website
   - managing employees
   - getting supplies
   - selling and shipping products
   - doing accounting and paying taxes

🎧 **Track 7** When saying large numbers, we use thought groups and intonation to make them easier for listeners to understand. Each numerical group in a large number ends with a rising intonation and slight pause except for the last group, which ends with falling intonation.

67,400   *sixty-seven thousand, four hundred*

3,011,382   *three million, eleven thousand, three hundred (and) eighty-two*

CRITICAL THINKING:
INTERPRETING
STATISTICS

E Work with a partner. Read the data below. Then ask and answer the questions. Remember to pronounce large numbers correctly.

2014 U.S. BUSINESS STATISTICS

- There were 5,825,458 businesses with paid employees.
- Small companies with under 500 employees represented 99.7 percent of employers.
- There were 19,076 large businesses.
- Small businesses employed almost half of the 121,069,944 workers.
- Small firms accounted for 63.3 percent of new jobs created between 1992 and 2013.

U.S. SMALL BUSINESS STATISTICS, 2009–2013

Category	2009	2010	2011	2012	2013
Start-ups	409,065	387,976	401,156	411,252	406,353
Closures	493,994	424,610	413,882	375,192	400,687
Bankruptcy[1]	58,721	58,322	49,895	44,435	36,061

Sources: Small Business Administration; U.S. Census Bureau

[1]**bankruptcy** (n): the legal state of being unable to pay bills

1. How many businesses with paid employees were there in the United States in 2014?
2. How many large businesses were there in 2014?
3. About how many workers were employed by small businesses in 2014?
4. Did the number of new business start-ups increase or decrease between 2009 and 2013? Why do you think this happened?
5. How many businesses in the United States closed in 2013? How does that number compare with 2009?
6. Did the number of bankruptcies increase or decrease between 2009 and 2013? How might you explain this?
7. What surprises or interests you about the statistics in the table? Why?

LESSON TASK Discussing Small Businesses

A Work with a partner. Discuss how each type of small business can benefit a
community. For example, can they provide employment, convenience, or a social
benefit? Think of examples in your own community.

CRITICAL THINKING:
EVALUATING

- Restaurants and coffee shops
- Retail shops (clothing, shoes, electronics, etc.)
- Manufacturers (windows, equipment, etc.)
- Service providers (auto repair, accountants, etc.)

B Discuss these questions with your partner and take notes on your ideas. Then together
organize and prepare a one-minute presentation.

ORGANIZING IDEAS

1. What kind of small business would you like to see open in your community? Why?
2. How many employees does this kind of business have? Do employees receive any job
   benefits, such as health insurance, employee discounts, or free meals?
3. Besides employment, what other benefits does the business provide to the
   community?
4. What statistics from page 10 can you use to support your ideas?

> *We would like to see a new grocery store open in our community. It would make food
> shopping more convenient, and it could employ around 25 people. In fact, small businesses
> created 63.3 percent of new jobs in the United States between 1992 and 2013.*

C With your partner, present your ideas from exercise B to another pair of students. As a
group, discuss the questions below.

PRESENTING

1. Which small business might bring the most benefits to the community?
2. Did numbers and statistics strengthen the presentations? What other numbers or
   statistics would have been useful to include?
3. If only one of the small businesses could open, which one would you choose? Why?

Second Shot Coffee in East London, U.K., founded by Julius
Ibrahim (left), employs people who are homeless. Customers
can purchase coffee or food for a person in need.

Video

A man and child sit under a light powered by a solar microgrid in a village near Jehanabad, Bihar, India.

Light for India's Villages

BEFORE VIEWING

A Work with a partner. Discuss the meanings of the terms you already know. Then fill in each blank with one of the words or phrases. You may use a dictionary to help you.

extend   infrastructure   kerosene   lack   working conditions

1. When you _____ something, you don't have enough of it.

2. The _____ of a place includes its physical structures such as buildings and roads.

3. When you _____ something, you make it bigger or make it include more.

4. You can burn _____ as a fuel.

5. Good _____ make it easier and healthier for people to do their jobs.

B The video is about a small power company that is bringing power to villages that are "off-grid"—without access to electricity. With a partner, list the daily challenges that are faced by people who live "off-grid."

WHILE VIEWING

C ▶ 1.2 Watch the video and write T for *True* or F for *False*. Correct the false statements.

UNDERSTANDING MAIN IDEAS

1. _____ The Terra Watt prize money is being used to supply electric power to rural villages.

2. _____ Some women's groups can now make products at night to sell in the market.

3. _____ People in rural villages used to spend very little money for kerosene or for cell-phone charging.

4. _____ A new microgrid from Mera Gao Power requires villages to give up some land.

D Which daily challenges that you listed in exercise B were mentioned in the video?

E ▶ 1.2 Watch the video again and fill in each blank with the number that you hear.

UNDERSTANDING DETAILS

1. Uttar Pradesh is a state of _____ people just to the east of New Delhi, with more than _____ percent off-grid.

2. In order to provide services to _____ homes, our technology is very simple.

3. Each one of our microgrids costs us about _____ dollars to provide service to a typical off-grid hamlet[1].

4. When Mera Gao Power completes the project under the Terra Watt Prize, we'll have connected _____ households in _____ villages.

[1]**hamlet** (n): a small village

AFTER VIEWING

> ### CRITICAL THINKING   Personalizing
>
> When you personalize information, you consider it in relation to your own life and experiences. Doing this can make the information more interesting to you and can help you to understand topics on a deeper level.

F Work in a small group. Complete these tasks.

CRITICAL THINKING: PERSONALIZING

1. Brainstorm a list of six or more ways you use electricity in your home. Then check the three things you would miss the most if you didn't have access to electricity.

2. Compare your list with the challenges you listed in exercise B. How is your use of electricity similar or different from that of the rural villagers in the video?

3. Mera Gao Power has received money from National Geographic and from investors, and in time, it will likely be a profitable company. If you were one of the owners, would you care more about the company's financial success or about its positive contributions to village life? Explain your answer.

Vocabulary

A 🎧 **Track 8** Listen and check (☞) the words you already know. Then discuss their meaning with a partner. Check the dictionary for any words you are not sure about.

☐ **accessible** (adj) ☐ **corporation** (n) ☐ **outcome** (n)
☐ **affordable** (adj) ☐ **demonstrate** (v) ☐ **response** (n)
☐ **charity** (n) ☐ **donate** (v)
☐ **concept** (n) ☐ **fundamental** (adj)

B Complete each statement with the correct form of a word from exercise A.

1. The _____ of keeping costs low and profits high is a(n) _____ idea for many businesses. They can't imagine doing business any other way.

2. The public _____ to the idea of space-tourism business has been mixed. Some people are eager to travel to space while others have no desire to go.

3. A(n) _____ is a large company such as Microsoft or BNP Paribas that meets a certain legal definition.

4. The hardware store plans to _____ part of its profits to a local _____ that helps people in need.

5. Many hospitals and clinics in India now have anti-venom so that lifesaving medicine is _____ to any person who lives near enough to those places.

6. The employees clearly _____ their community spirit by actively volunteering in a wide variety of community events.

7. For companies that want to make the world a better place, looking at profits is not the only way to measure a successful _____. It's also important to look at the difference the company has made in people's lives.

8. A product or service usually needs to be _____ in order to be successful. If it is too expensive, many people will not buy it.

▶ **Shivani Siroya, shown with her California team, founded InVenture to help people in developing countries establish credit and get loans. They provide personal data about people who want to start a small business.**

C Track 9 Read the information and fill in each blank with a word from exercise A. Then listen and check your answers.

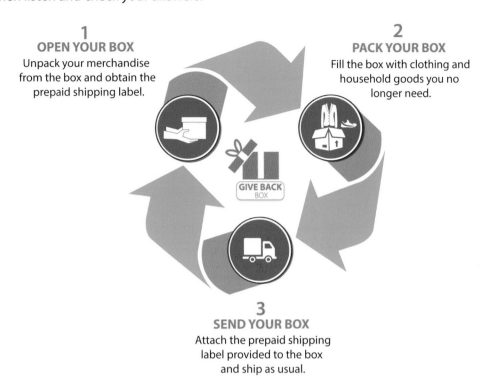

1
OPEN YOUR BOX
Unpack your merchandise from the box and obtain the prepaid shipping label.

2
PACK YOUR BOX
Fill the box with clothing and household goods you no longer need.

3
SEND YOUR BOX
Attach the prepaid shipping label provided to the box and ship as usual.

GIVE BACK BOX

THE GIVE BACK BOX

The _____ behind the Give Back Box is pretty simple. When someone
1
receives a box from an online retailer such as Amazon or Overstock, they can fill

it with clothing or household goods they want to _____. Using a free
2

shipping label, the box is shipped to a local _____ where the goods are
3

sold at very _____ prices or given away for free to people who need them.
4

Give Back Box itself is not a charitable organization. They're a for-profit company,

but one of their _____ goals is to do more than make money. Founder
5

Monika Wiela sees the company as a way to help people in need and, at the same

time, help online companies _____ their social responsibility[1]. So far, the
6

_____ from customers has been good. They're eager to help others by
7

donating goods, and they're happy to reuse their cardboard boxes as well.

[1]**social responsibility** (n ph.) the concept of businesses making positive contributions to society

D Discuss these questions with a partner.   PERSONALIZING

1. Would you use a service such as the Give Back Box? Why or why not?

2. Many people have more clothing, furniture, and other goods than they need. What are some ways to make these goods accessible to people who really need them?

Listening A Meeting about Social Responsibility

BEFORE LISTENING

PERSONALIZING **A** Work with a partner. Look at the statistics. Then discuss the questions below.

> **Consumers' Attitudes about Corporate Social Responsibility (CSR)**
>
> 93% have a more positive opinion of companies that demonstrate CSR
> 90% would decide to purchase or not based on companies' CSR practices
> 88% are more loyal to companies that practice CSR
> 80% would tell friends and family about a company's CSR efforts
> 72% believe their purchases have some impact on social or environmental issues

1. Which of these statements are true for you? Explain.
2. Which statistic is the most surprising to you? Why?

WHILE LISTENING

LISTENING FOR
MAIN IDEAS **B** 🎧 **Track 10** Listen to the meeting and take notes to complete the chart.

	Type of Company	How Are They Socially Responsible?
1.		
2.		

LISTENING SKILL Listening for Similarities and Contrasts

Listening for expressions such as the ones below will help you understand whether two ideas, things, or people are similar in some way or are different.

Similarity: *also*   *too*   *both*   *as well*   *the same*

> *Jason and I had **the same** idea. We were **both** thinking about opening a cafe.*

Contrast: *although*   *though*   *even though*   *but*   *yet*

> ***Although** it is a small company, it makes a big difference in the community. How could our company do some good, **yet** still make a profit?*

C 🎧 **Track 11** Listen to excerpts from the meeting and fill in each blank with the word(s) you hear. Then with a partner, discuss whether each excerpt shows a similarity or contrast.

LISTENING FOR SIMILARITIES AND CONTRASTS

1. One is a huge drug manufacturer, and this one looks like a small company that makes handbags and backpacks. They _____ seem to be very different from our company.

2. That's interesting, _____ surprising as well. I thought they were just interested in making a profit.

3. Their customers like the idea of doing something to help kids, and State Bags is doing well as a business, especially for a young company. That's the kind of outcome we're looking for, _____ .

4. _____ we're a small company, we can still make a difference. Why don't we do some brainstorming?

AFTER LISTENING

D Discuss the questions with a partner.

CRITICAL THINKING: EVALUATING

1. The two companies mentioned in the meeting are doing very different things. How much social good do you think their different actions accomplish? Explain.

2. At the end of the meeting, you hear a suggestion for a brainstorm session to think of ways the software engineering firm could become more socially responsible and still make a profit. Which of the actions below might have the most impact? Explain.

   a. reducing the company's use of paper in its daily operations
   b. providing free software to help local charities manage their operations
   c. offering a free after-school software development class for high school students

Volunteers help prepare backpacks for school children in New York City, USA.

MAKING A LIVING, MAKING A DIFFERENCE **17**

B Speaking

GRAMMAR FOR SPEAKING Indirect Questions

An indirect question is a question inside another question or statement. We use indirect questions because they are often more polite than direct questions.

> *What are these companies doing?*   (direct question)
> **Can you please explain** <u>what</u> *these companies are doing?*   (indirect question)

Indirect questions begin with a polite phrase and use the word order for statements, not questions. Here are some other phrases we use for indirect questions.

> **Do you know** <u>whether/if</u> *the company is socially responsible?*
> **Can you tell me** <u>how</u> *the box recycling program works?*
> **Could you explain** <u>why</u> *you chose these particular companies?*

Indirect questions can also be in the form of statements. These are less polite but common.

> **I'm wondering** <u>why</u> *you chose these two companies.*
> **I'd like to know** <u>how</u> *people make a living selling snake venom.*

A Work with a partner. Change the questions to indirect questions. Then practice asking and answering them.

1. What time is it?

   _____

2. Why are you taking this class?

   _____

3. How old were you when you took your first English class?

   _____

4. What kind of career do you hope to have in the future?

   _____

5. How do you make decisions about the clothing you buy?

   _____

6. Where should I go for a day trip this weekend?

   _____

EVERYDAY LANGUAGE Showing Interest

More formal: *How interesting. Is that right? I didn't know that.*

Less formal: *Wow! Really? That's amazing. That's great.*

B Change each question to an indirect question. Then ask and answer the questions with a partner, continuing each conversation as long as possible. Remember to show interest in what your partner says.

1. What is the most influential technology company?
2. How do people get jobs with good companies?
3. Would you want to be a member of a cooperative?
4. What kind of small business would you like to start?

C Read each statement. Choose if it is true for you or not. Then change the false statements to be true for you.

1.	I would like to start my own business someday.	T	F
2.	If I had my own business, I would donate some of my profits to charity.	T	F
3.	I would like to work for a large corporation.	T	F
4.	I would prefer to work for a small business.	T	F
5.	I would like to raise children and be a homemaker.	T	F
6.	I already have some work experience.	T	F
7.	I'd rather have an affordable lifestyle and not work long hours.	T	F
8.	I'd prefer to work longer hours and have more money to spend.	T	F

D Work with a partner. Share and explain your answers from exercise C. Then discuss these questions about your work-related dreams for the future. Ask indirect questions to get more information and use expressions to show interest.

1. What do you think is the most appropriate kind of career for you? Why do you think so?
2. What is your dream job?

A: *Can you tell me why you think a new bakery would be successful in your hometown?*
B: *Sure. It's because two bakeries have closed in recent years. Now there is no place to buy fresh bread and cakes, and most people don't have time to bake those things themselves.*

FINAL TASK Presenting a Socially Responsible Business

> You are going to research a business that is socially responsible and give a presentation about it.

A For the topic of your presentation, choose a business that you know or that you want to learn more about. Locate the business's website and follow these steps.

1. Read general information about the company on the "About Us" page. Take notes.
2. Look for information about its corporate social responsibility. This may be under "Social Responsibility," "Mission," or "Values."
3. Write down three interesting facts about the company, and three interesting facts about its social responsibility efforts.

PRESENTATION SKILL Looking Up While Speaking

When speaking in front of a large group, it is important to connect with your audience. One way to do this is by looking up and making eye contact. Try to look down at your notes only occasionally, and then look up and speak. When you look at the audience, look at different members of the audience, including those close to you and those in the back of the room.

B Practice your presentation. Use the notes you took in exercise A and your own words to talk about the business you researched. Practice looking up while speaking.

PRESENTING **C** Give your presentation to a small group of students. Remember to look up from your notes while you are speaking. Answer any questions your classmates might have.

REFLECTION

1. What did you learn about using numbers and statistics in this unit?

_____

_____

2. What topics from the unit were the most interesting to you? Why?

_____

_____

3. Here are the vocabulary words from the unit. Check (✓) the ones you can use.

☐ accessible AWL	☐ corporation AWL	☐ generate AWL
☐ affordable	☐ demonstrate AWL	☐ model
☐ assess AWL	☐ diverse AWL	☐ outcome AWL
☐ charity	☐ donate	☐ poverty
☐ concept AWL	☐ effective	☐ profit
☐ conventional AWL	☐ entrepreneur	☐ response AWL
☐ cooperate AWL	☐ fundamental AWL	

TRADITIONAL AND MODERN MEDICINE

2

A man undergoes cryotherapy in New York, NY, USA. Cryotherapy, which is the use of very cold temperatures for medical treatment, was used as early as the 17th century.

ACADEMIC SKILLS

LISTENING	Listening for Supporting Details
	Indenting Details
SPEAKING	Using Phrases to Signal Reasons
	Linking Vowel Sounds with /y/ and /w/
CRITICAL THINKING	Evaluating Claims

THINK AND DISCUSS

1 Look at the picture. What do you imagine cold-temperature therapy is good for?
2 What other traditional therapies are still in use today?

Look at the photos and read the information. Then discuss the questions.

1. What information on this page surprises you?
2. What experiences have you had with these or other home remedies?
3. What are some differences between traditional medicine and modern medicine?

HOME REMEDIES

Lavender contains an oil that may have calming effects and relax muscles. More research is being done to determine the science behind its effects.

Garlic has long been used as a natural remedy. Garlic may reduce the frequency of colds, and it has possible cardiovascular benefits. Garlic oil has been used as a mosquito repellent.

▶ Chili peppers have been used for health purposes for thousands of years. Chilis can be used as a decongestant. Capsaicin, a compound in chilis, is thought to increase life-span and help cure some kinds of cancer.

▶ Ginger is an effective remedy for nausea and vomiting, according to research. This root contains anti-inflammatory elements that can help relieve a sore throat.

A Vocabulary

MEANING FROM CONTEXT **A** 🎧 **Track 12** Read and listen to the information. Notice each word in blue and think about its meaning.

PLANT-BASED MEDICINES

Using plants as natural **remedies** for health problems is nothing new. In fact, for some people, medicinal plants are the only affordable and available kind of medicine. When these people become ill, they discuss their **symptoms** with a traditional healer rather than a medical doctor. Now some scientists want drug manufacturers to take a new look at the ability of plants to **restore** health and fight diseases such as cancer.

Rosy periwinkle

Root of chicory plant

Nat Quansah, an ethnobotanist in Madagascar, studies plants such as the rosy periwinkle. A **synthetic** version of the chemical from that plant is now made into drugs that **inhibit** cancer growth. These drugs have dramatically increased survival rates for two kinds of childhood cancer.

Jim Duke, retired from the U.S. Department of Agriculture, grows and writes about medicinal plants such as chicory. Chicory contains chicoric acid, which could be useful in fighting a deadly virus[1]. Duke says that **empirical** studies of medicinal plants are **crucial** to developing new medicines.

PROBLEMS WITH PLANT-BASED MEDICINES

The effectiveness of a medicine can be difficult to study scientifically. One reason for this is that sick people who use a medicine and then recover may **associate** their recovery correctly or incorrectly with its effects. In addition, herbal remedies may not be **consistent** because the amounts of natural chemicals in plants can vary significantly. The **variables** include the soil plants are grown in and the time when they are harvested, among other factors.

[1]**virus** (n): a tiny organism that causes diseases such as influenza and the common cold

B Write each word in blue from exercise A next to its definition.

1. _____ (n) medicines or things that make us feel better
2. _____ (adj) repeated in the same way
3. _____ (adj) based on scientific observations and experiments
4. _____ (adj) extremely important
5. _____ (v) to connect or relate two things
6. _____ (v) to slow or prevent
7. _____ (v) to return to its original condition
8. _____ (n) factors in a situation
9. _____ (adj) artificial; human-made
10. _____ (n) signs of illness

C Discuss the questions with a partner.

1. When was the last time you were sick? What were your symptoms? What medicines or remedies did you use?
2. Why are empirical studies important when developing medicines based on plants?
3. Name two habits that are crucial to good health. Do you have these habits? Explain.
4. After a natural disaster, communities try to restore medical services as soon as possible. What other services would be important to restore quickly?
5. Do you think your parents were consistent or inconsistent with the way they set rules when you were growing up? Why do you think so?
6. Think of a time you were successful. What feelings do you associate with that time? Explain.

VOCABULARY SKILL Word Families

A word family includes words that share the same root. A root gives a word its meaning. For example, the root *var* (from Latin) means "change." Suffixes added to the root indicate the part of speech. Learning about the members of word families can help you to build your vocabulary.

Verb	Noun	Adjective	Adverb
vary	*variation, variable, variability, variety*	*variable, varied, various*	*variably*

D Use a dictionary to complete the word-family chart. Then with a partner, create sentences with each word.

Verb	Noun	Adjective	Adverb
restore			X
X		consistent	
inhibit			X

Listening A Lecture about Plant-Based Medicines

BEFORE LISTENING

A With a partner, look at the steps in the development of a new medication under the U.S. Food and Drug Administration (FDA). Then discuss the questions.

1. Which steps usually take place in a laboratory? Which seem to focus on a new medication's safety? On its effectiveness?

2. How much time would you guess this process typically takes? Explain.

The Drug Development Process

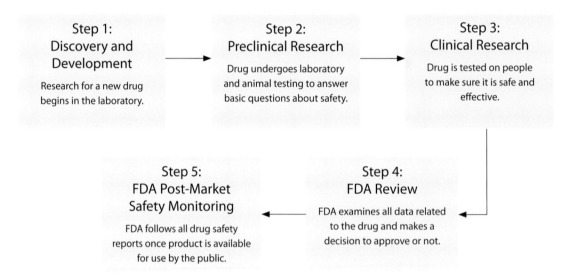

Step 1:
Discovery and Development

Research for a new drug begins in the laboratory.

Step 2:
Preclinical Research

Drug undergoes laboratory and animal testing to answer basic questions about safety.

Step 3:
Clinical Research

Drug is tested on people to make sure it is safe and effective.

Step 5:
FDA Post-Market Safety Monitoring

FDA follows all drug safety reports once product is available for use by the public.

Step 4:
FDA Review

FDA examines all data related to the drug and makes a decision to approve or not.

WHILE LISTENING

B 🎧 **Track 13** ▶ **2.1** Listen to the lecture. Check (✓) the points that the professor makes.

☐ a. Many useful older medications were based on plants.

☐ b. A new plant-based drug is being used to treat people with diabetes.

☐ c. Two new drugs are effective at fighting cancer in children.

☐ d. Plant-based medicines are made directly from plants or from synthetic versions of the chemicals found in plants.

☐ e. The path from discovery to government approval is quicker with plant-based medicines than with completely synthetic medicines.

When you are taking notes, it's helpful to have a visual way to distinguish main ideas from details. Indenting the details makes your notes easier to read and understand.

> *Main idea 1…*
> > *Detail 1…*
> > *Detail 2…*

C 🎧 **Track 13** Read through the partial notes. Then listen again and complete the notes. Notice that the details are indented to distinguish them from the main ideas.

LISTENING FOR DETAILS

Many useful older meds _____

    Aspirin: chem. found in _____

    Digoxin: heart disease med. from _____

Another plant: rosy periwinkle

    Traditional: used for people with _____

    New: _____

Meds. not made directly from plants

    _____ chemical in plant

    Synthesize chemical in _____

New plant-based meds: Devel. is long, $$ process b/c many variables.

1. Study effect'ness of trad. remedy.

2. Plant variables: e.g., picked wrong _____ of plant, picked at wrong _____ , effect of other plants growing nearby.

3. Scientists need to know _____ is active and what _____ to put in each tablet, injection, etc.

Overall, devel. of synthetic drugs is _____

AFTER LISTENING

D Work with a partner. Use your notes from exercise C to explain the ideas from the lecture in your own words to your partner. Then switch roles.

Speaking

GRAMMAR FOR SPEAKING Adverb Clauses of Reason and Purpose

Adverb clauses of reason and purpose tell us why something happens.

      main clause   adverb clause

People use medicinal plants <u>because they are available and affordable</u>.

Scientists study home remedies <u>so that they can identify possible new medications</u>.

We introduce adverb clauses of reason with *because* and *since*. Notice that the adverb clause can come before or after the main clause.

> **<u>Because</u>** *<u>the amounts of natural chemicals in plants can vary significantly</u>, herbal remedies may not be consistent.*

> *Native Americans used to chew the tree bark **<u>since</u>** <u>it relieved pain</u>.*

We introduce adverb clauses of purpose with *so (that)*.

> *Those chemicals are taken from the foxglove plant **so (that)** they can be used to make a medication to treat heart patients.*

A Work with a partner. Match each sentence beginning to its ending. Then discuss the relationship between the clauses. Which clause explains why something happens?

1. I eat fruits and vegetables _____.
2. Because plants are affordable, _____.
3. Scientists study a plant _____.
4. Since aspirin is easily available, _____.
5. Plants can be difficult to study _____.

  a. many people use it to relieve pain
  b. so that they can understand its properties
  c. because they're a crucial part of a good diet
  d. since there are many variables involved
  e. many people use them as remedies

B Complete each statement so that it is true for you. Then share your statements with a partner. Ask and answer follow-up questions about the statements.

1. I (sometimes / rarely) visit the doctor because _____.

2. I (use / don't use) natural remedies because _____

_____.

3. I (have / don't have) a positive view of plant-based medicines since _____

_____.

4. Since I am (not) very healthy, I _____.

5. So that I can be as healthy as possible, I _____.

6. Because I learned about plant-based medicines in this unit, I _____

_____.

A: *I rarely visit the doctor because I am pretty healthy.*
B: *How do you stay healthy? What's your secret?*

◀ **Feliciano dos Santos performs in a concert.**

C 🎧 Track 14 Read and listen to information about a National Geographic Explorer. How is he making his country a healthier place?

> **FIGHTING DISEASE WITH A GUITAR**
>
> As a child in Mozambique's Niassa Province, Feliciano dos Santos caught the polio virus from the dirty water in his tiny village. The disease affected his ability to walk. "When I was young," he recalls, "I never believed I would grow up, get married, have children, drive a car, and live such a full life."
>
> These days, dos Santos and his band *Massukos* use music to spread messages of sanitation and hygiene[1] to some of the poorest, most remote villages in Mozambique. Their hit song, "Wash Your Hands," is part of a public health campaign created by dos Santos's non-governmental organization (NGO), Estamos.
>
> Dos Santos's NGO also works on programs to install pumps for clean water, conduct health studies, and fight infectious diseases. Says dos Santos, "Clean water is a basic human right, yet so many don't have it. I'm using my music to be the voice of people who have no voice."

[1]**sanitation; hygiene** (n): cleanliness

D With your partner, use these words and phrases to write statements with adverb clauses of reason and purpose. Use the information from exercise C and your own ideas.

1. Dos Santos / not expect / live a full life / because

   _____

2. Since / Massukos's health message / in a popular song / pay attention

   _____

3. So that / more people / have clean water / dos Santos's NGO

   _____

E Discuss these questions with a partner.

1. Describe public health campaigns you have seen or heard about. For example, what TV commercials or outdoor signs with health messages have you seen?
2. Do you think a popular song would work well in a public health campaign in your country? Give reasons for your opinion using adverb clauses.

SPEAKING SKILL Using Phrases to Signal Reasons

We sometimes use a phrase at the beginning of a statement to let our listeners know that we are giving a reason for something.

For this reason, …   *Because of this, …*   *That is why…*   *That's the reason…*

Diseases can spread from person to person through dirty water. **That is why** *it's crucially important to use clean water for drinking and cooking.*

F Work with a partner. Follow each statement below with one or more new statements that contain a reason. Try to use all four phrases from the box.

1. The common cold is highly contagious and spreads easily.
2. We associate regular exercise with good health.
3. Some natural remedies are quite effective.
4. A good diet contributes to overall health.

CRITICAL THINKING:
EVALUATING

G Follow these steps with your partner.

1. Look at the list of health issues in the chart below. Which information surprises you the most. Why?
2. Brainstorm some of the public health issues in your country. Examples might include tobacco use, sanitation, diet, air quality, and so on. Which one is the most concerning? Give reasons.
3. Join another pair of students and discuss which issues are the most serious.

Public Health in the United States: The Top Four Concerns	
Diabetes (high blood-sugar levels)	– 8.3 percent of Americans have diabetes
Obesity (being very overweight)	– 38 percent of American adults are obese
Heart disease	– Causes around 25 percent of deaths
Cancer	– Second leading cause of death in the United States

H With a partner, think of a title of a new song that could be used to spread a message about one of the issues you discussed in exercise G. Then share your ideas in a group.

LESSON TASK   Discussing Claims about Public Health

> **CRITICAL THINKING**   Evaluating Claims
>
> A claim is a statement that is presented as true. It should be logical and be supported with evidence such as research of some kind. A claim may also use tentative language (*suggests*, *may be*, *can*) to show that the claim is not an absolute or undeniable truth.
>
> *A recent study suggests that air quality may be the worst threat to public health in this city.*

A Work in a small group and evaluate the claims below. Discuss these questions to help you decide if each claim is strong.

CRITICAL THINKING: EVALUATING CLAIMS

1. Does the person provide statistics, research results, expert opinions, or some other evidence that I can trust?
2. Is the claim reasonable and logical based on what I know?
3. Is the claim current, or is it outdated or based on outdated evidence?
4. Does the person have anything to gain by making the claim?
5. How would you rank these claims from 1 (most believable) to 3 (least believable)?

> a. *Our dentists are the best in the region, and good dental care is the basis of good health. Give us a call and let Southwest Dentists take care of your teeth.*
>   Andrea Walker, Outreach Director, Southwest Dentists Associated
>
> b. *A 2016 study published in* The New England Journal of Medicine *found that the meningitis B vaccine[1] was only effective in around two-thirds of the college students who received it. However, since the disease can cause death, we strongly recommend the vaccine for all students aged 17–21.*
>   Luigi Maglio, chancellor of a large public university
>
> c. *Absent workers cost U.S. companies over $225 billion a year according to the Center for Disease Control's 2015 report. Don't wait for your employees to call in sick. Call us about our employee wellness program. You're in Good Company.*
>   Max Rosas, Sales and Marketing Director, Good Company Health Solutions

[1] **vaccine** (n): a medicine that stimulates the body's immune system to protect against a disease

B With your group, discuss how you would support the claims below. Explain your reasons.

> Types of support:
>
> statistics   expert opinions   personal stories   other

1. Fewer children have gotten malaria since the new water wells were installed.
2. Adults are often more afraid of getting injections than children are.
3. Reducing salt intake lessens the likelihood of heart disease.
4. Parents noticed unusual symptoms after their children received the new flu vaccine.

Video

Wild Health

BEFORE VIEWING

A The video you are going to watch, *Wild Health*, discusses what animals do to self-medicate, or cure themselves, when they are sick or injured. What are some things you think animals might do to self-medicate? List two ideas below.

_____   _____

B Work with a partner. Write each word or phrase from the video next to its definition. You may use a dictionary.

avoidance	curative	groundbreaking	nausea
compounds	fermentation	lactation	preventative

1. _____ (adj) helping to keep disease away

2. _____ (n) a chemical change to a substance

3. _____ (n) substances that consist of two or more elements

4. _____ (adj) able to restore health

5. _____ (n) the condition of feeling sick to your stomach

6. _____ (n) the production of milk by female mammals

7. _____ (n) the act of staying away from something

8. _____ (adj) innovative and important

WHILE VIEWING

C ▶ 2.2 Watch the video and complete the notes.

1. Cindy Engel, animal behaviorist, studies zoopharmacognosy (means "animal

   _____")

2. Acc. to Engel, _____ was based on watching sick animals

   e.g., _____ have shown us 6–7 new compounds to use

3. Engel's book focuses on 3 main areas:

   curative measures (_____ can cure ailments themselves)

   _____ measures (animals do something to protect against illness)

   _____ measures (not eating certain foods)

D ▶ 2.2 Engel uses different animals as examples to support her research. Watch the video again. Match each animal with the correct example.

1. Chimpanzees _____.

2. Snow leopards _____.

3. Wildebeests _____.

4. Cattle/cows _____.

a. eat grass to avoid nausea

b. migrate to places that have essential minerals for lactation

c. travel to find the right kind of dirt

d. have helped scientists discover several new compounds

AFTER VIEWING

E Discuss the questions below in a group.

1. Which of your predictions from exercise A were mentioned in the video?
2. Based on what you learned in Lesson A about evaluating claims, what do you think of Engel's claim that observing animal behavior is important to human medicine? Is it a believable claim? Why or why not?

A pair of young chimpanzees in the Republic of the Congo

Vocabulary

A 🎧 **Track 15** Read and listen to the information. Notice each word in **blue** and think about its meaning.

HIGH-TECH MEDICINE

Science fiction writers in the 1960s imagined the "tricorder." The **radical** idea behind the device was its ability to scan the body from the outside and "see" everything from tiny bacteria to **internal** organs such as the heart. This meant patients didn't need to **undergo** surgery or other invasive procedures in order to get a medical diagnosis—in fictional stories, at least. Now, the tricorder idea might soon be a reality, and could be used by patients to monitor their own health or by doctors in places far from hospitals.

In the area of regenerative medicine, researchers are using 3-D printing techniques to create replacement body tissues. This synthetic nose was created by Dr. Anthony Atala at the Wake Forest Institute for Regenerative Medicine in North Carolina, USA. Scientists are also working on ways to get the body's own cells and immune system to **modify** parts of the human body for use in surgical repairs. For example, the body could generate new knee cartilage[1] that will be accepted more easily than a completely artificial knee **mechanism**.

[1]**cartilage** (n): firm, flexible tissue found in several parts of the body

B Work with a partner. Read the statements aloud and discuss whether you think they are true or false. Choose T for *True* or F for *False*. Correct the false statements.

1. If someone has a radical idea, it is similar to what many others think.　　T　F

2. An internal medical device is located on the outside of the body.　　T　F

3. If you undergo surgery, the surgery is done to you.　　T　F

4. When you modify something, you change it or give it a different form.　　T　F

5. A mechanism is a mechanical device with a certain function.　　T　F

C ⌂ **Track 16** Read and listen to the information. Notice each word in **blue** and think about its meaning.

MEANING FROM CONTEXT

> ### NEW ADVANCES IN PROSTHETIC DEVICES[1]
>
> - A prosthetic device can help restore movement for a person who has suffered a **severe** injury and has lost a leg, an arm, a foot, or a hand.
>
> - Advanced prosthetic arms can now be operated mentally. The user thinks about moving her hand, for example, and the **corresponding** part of the device moves.
>
> - After a patient loses an arm, **nerves** that once went to the patient's arm are surgically attached to the remaining **muscles**. The nerves move the muscles, which **transmit** electrical signals to the prosthetic arm.

[1]**prosthetic devices** (n): artificial devices that take the place of a body part such as a hand or leg

D Write each word in **blue** from exercise C next to its definition.

1. _____ (n) tissue in the body that allows feeling or sensation

2. _____ (adj) bad, causing great damage

3. _____ (v) to send a signal or message

4. _____ (n) tissues on bones that make the body move

5. _____ (adj) matching

E Read each sentence and choose the correct word form. You may use a dictionary to help you.

1. When we sneeze or cough, we may (transmit / transmission) a disease to people around us.
2. Some medicines are applied to the skin, while other medicines need to be taken (internal / internally).
3. In an emergency, a simple (modify / modification) can make a medical device for an adult work well for a child.
4. Signals that allow us to see and hear travel across (nerves / nervous) inside the head.
5. Before a strenuous workout, it is a good idea to warm up your (muscles / muscular) with gentle stretches.

F Work in a small group and discuss these questions.

PERSONALIZING

1. Do you know anyone who has a prosthetic device such as an artificial knee, hip joint, or leg? Explain.
2. What ideas or feelings do you have about these examples of high-tech medicine—the "tricorder" device, regenerative medicine, and advanced prosthetic devices? For example, would you feel comfortable taking advantage of such medical science?
3. Do you feel optimistic about the future of medicine? Give reasons for your answers.

B Listening A Podcast about Prosthetic Devices

Amanda Kitts trains her prosthetic arm with a computer system in a clinic in Chicago, Illinois, USA.

BEFORE LISTENING

A Discuss these questions with a partner.

1. How do you think Amanda Kitts controls the prosthetic arm you see her wearing in the photo? What movements do you think are hard for the arm to make?
2. How would you go through your morning routine if you had only one arm? For example, how would you brush your teeth? Bathe and dress yourself? Make and eat breakfast? Discuss the steps involved in these activities and how they would be different from what you normally do.

WHILE LISTENING

LISTENING FOR
MAIN IDEAS

B 🎧 **Track 17** Read the questions. Then listen to the podcast and answer the questions.

1. How were older prosthetic arms operated?

_____

_____

2. What other kind of prosthetic device is mentioned, and what does it do?

_____

_____

3. How is the body modified in targeted reinnervation surgery?

_____

_____

4. How do electrodes work to make Kitts's prosthetic arm move?

_____

_____

LISTENING SKILL Listening for Supporting Details

Supporting details often include examples, an explanation of a process, numerical data, research results, and the ideas of experts. Notice how the details in bold in these sentences help us understand and trust the speakers' points.

> _Natural remedies are a common way to deal with minor health problems, for example, **drinking hot tea with honey** to ease the symptoms of a cold._

> _Targeted reinnervation surgery was developed at the **Rehabilitation Institute of Chicago. Dr. Todd Kuiken and Dr. Gregory Dumanium** are the innovative surgeons behind the technique._

C 🎧 **Track 17** Listen again and take notes on these supporting details.

LISTENING FOR DETAILS

1. How Amanda Kitts lost her arm:

_____

2. Number of people with cochlear implants:

_____

3. What doctors do in targeted reinnervation surgery:

_____

4. How Kitts's muscles make the prosthetic arm move:

_____

5. The role Kitts's brain plays in moving the prosthetic arm:

_____

AFTER LISTENING

D With a partner, discuss how the details you took notes on in exercise C helped you to understand or believe the information in the podcast.

CRITICAL THINKING: APPLYING

> _Hearing the number of people with cochlear implants helped me see that it's a very common high-tech prosthetic device. It's not something out of science fiction._

E Discuss these questions with your partner.

1. What information from the podcast surprised you the most? Why?
2. What questions would you ask Amanda Kitts if you had the chance to speak with her?

B Speaking

🎧 **Track 18** When words that end in /i/ or /aɪ/ are followed by words that begin with a vowel sound, we can link the words together with a /y/ sound for smoother and more fluent pronunciation.

> "We always" sounds like "Weyalways."
>
> "I am" sounds like "Iyam."

With words that end in /o/ and /u/, we can link to words that begin with a vowel sound by using a /w/ sound.

> "So easy" sounds like "Soweasy."
>
> "Who is" sounds like "Whowis."

A 🎧 **Track 19** Listen and choose the sound that links the words in each sentence. Then practice saying the sentences with a partner using linking.

1. She is not getting a radical kind of surgery.   /y/   /w/

2. Who else in your family has flu symptoms?   /y/   /w/

3. He asked about the new medication.   /y/   /w/

4. They did two other blood tests.   /y/   /w/

5. Three of his friends are sick.   /y/   /w/

6. Why isn't he undergoing the operation?   /y/   /w/

▶ Aiden Kenny got two cochlear implants when he was ten months old. The implants transmit electronic signals directly to his auditory nerves and allow him to perceive sounds. Within months of the surgery, Aiden spoke the words "Mama" and "Dada."

B 🎧 **Track 20** Listen to the conversation. Pay attention to the words linked with /y/ and /w/ sounds. Then practice the conversation with a partner.

A: How are you doing today?
B: I'm good, thanks. I was just listening to an incredible story about cochlear implants.
A: Sounds interesting. I always enjoy stories about new medical developments.
B: Me too! This was about a deaf child who got the implants when he was very young. His parents wanted him to be able to hear and speak normally.
A: That must have been a tough decision for the parents to make.
B: I imagine so. Well, it was nice seeing you.

EVERYDAY LANGUAGE   Ending a Conversation

To end a conversation politely, you can start with a signal word, give an explanation, and suggest a future plan.

Signal Word	Explanation	Future Plan
Well,	*I need to get going.*	*Give me a call tonight if you're not busy.*
So,	*my next class starts at 11:00.*	*I'll see you tomorrow at work.*
Anyway,	*it was nice talking to you.*	*Let's get together for coffee one of these days.*

C Think of some recent news you read or heard related to medical inventions or health news. Have a short conversation with a partner, sharing the news that you know. At the end, close the conversation politely.

D Work with a different partner.

A: *What's new with you, Marco?*
B: *Not much, but I read an interesting news article this morning.*

FINAL TASK A Presentation on Medicine and Health

> You are going to give a short presentation about one of the topics from this unit that interested you or about another topic related to medicine and health.

A Work with a partner. Discuss what you learned about these topics. Brainstorm other topics related to health that interest you and add them.

BRAINSTORMING

- a traditional medicine
- a recent advance in high-tech medicine
- _____

- a plant-based medicine
- a specific prosthetic device
- _____

B Choose a topic from your brainstorm in exercise A and follow these steps.

1. Find an article or news story about your topic. It should be written for the general public and easy to understand.
2. Take notes on main ideas and supporting details as you read the article. Pay attention to the reasons that are given.
3. Plan a short (2-3 minute) presentation to give to your classmates.

PRESENTATION SKILL Practicing and Timing Your Presentation

Before giving a presentation, practice it several times and make sure the length is suitable. Practicing with a friend or in front of a mirror lets you work out effective ways to phrase your ideas, and timing yourself ensures that your presentation won't be too long or too short.

Many people speak faster when they feel nervous, so their actual presentation takes less time than they expected. If you tend to speak too quickly, remind yourself to speak slowly and carefully during your presentation. This will help your listeners understand you and will give them time to think about your ideas.

C Practice and time your presentation. Try to speak in a natural way rather than reading directly from your notes. Remember to use phrases to signal reasons.

D In a small group, give your presentation and listen to other presentations. Give each other feedback on the timing and delivery of your presentations.

REFLECTION

1. What two skills from the unit will be the most useful to you?

   _____

   _____

2. What were the most interesting things you learned about traditional and modern medicine in this unit?

   _____

   _____

3. Here are the vocabulary words from the unit. Check (✓) the ones you can use.

   ☐ associate   ☐ mechanism AWL   ☐ severe

   ☐ consistent AWL   ☐ modify AWL   ☐ symptom

   ☐ corresponding AWL   ☐ muscle   ☐ synthetic

   ☐ crucial AWL   ☐ nerve   ☐ transmit AWL

   ☐ empirical AWL   ☐ radical AWL   ☐ undergo AWL

   ☐ inhibit AWL   ☐ remedy   ☐ variable AWL

   ☐ internal AWL   ☐ restore AWL

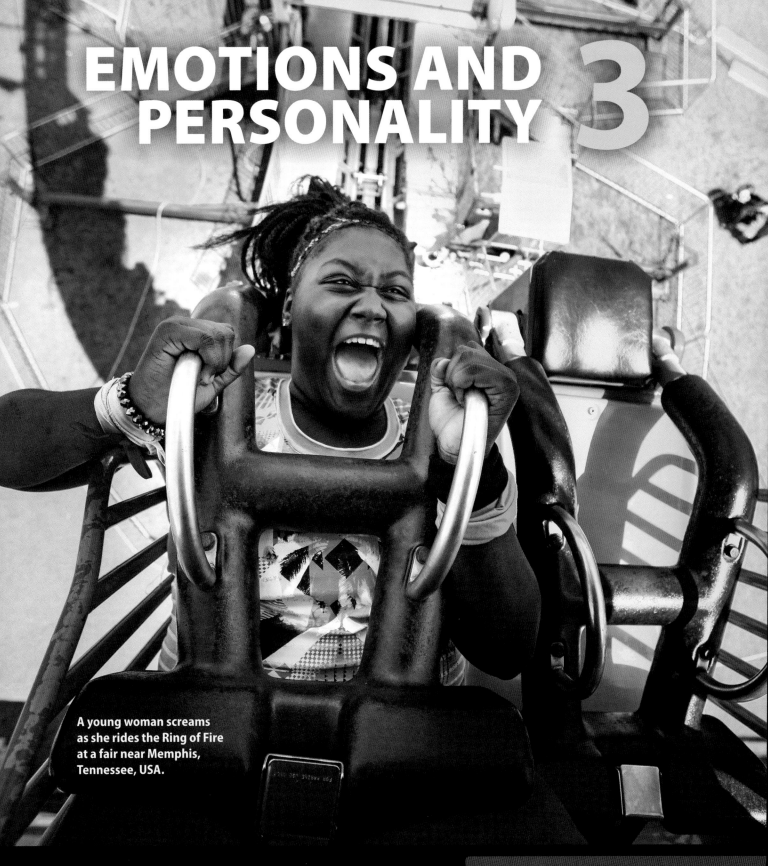

EMOTIONS AND PERSONALITY 3

A young woman screams as she rides the Ring of Fire at a fair near Memphis, Tennessee, USA.

ACADEMIC SKILLS

LISTENING — Listening for Consequences
Using a Word Web

SPEAKING — Defending an Opinion
Using Punctuation Marks

CRITICAL THINKING — Making Judgments

THINK AND DISCUSS

1 What emotions do you think this woman is feeling?
2 When is the last time you screamed like this? What made you scream?

Look at the photo and read the information. Then discuss the questions.

1. Why do you imagine that this couple feels so happy?

2. What is most surprising to you about the Gallup Positive Experience Survey results?

3. How would you answer each of the questions in the Positive Experience Index?

THE GLOBAL STATE OF EMOTIONS

Where are the happiest people in the world?

The Gallup Positive Experience Poll includes the results from surveys conducted around the world. In the Positive Experience Index, people were surveyed about the feelings and emotions during their daily experiences. The results give a snapshot of our global state of emotions.

A man celebrates his 100th birthday with his wife and family in Ñeembucú, Paraguay.

Gallup Positive Experience Poll

Positive Experience Index Questions

- Did you feel well-rested yesterday?

- Were you treated with respect all day yesterday?

- Did you smile or laugh a lot yesterday?

- Did you learn or do something interesting yesterday?

- Did you experience enjoyment during a lot of the day yesterday?

Survey Results

- The Gallup Positive Experience Poll was conducted in 142 countries in 2016.

- More than 70 percent of people worldwide said they experienced a lot of enjoyment, smiled or laughed a lot, felt well-rested, and felt treated with respect.

- Fifty-one percent of people said they learned or did something interesting the day before the interview.

- Paraguay had the highest percentage of people reporting positive experiences.

- The top eleven countries were: Paraguay, Costa Rica, Panama, the Philippines, Uzbekistan, Ecuador, Guatemala, Mexico, Norway, Chile, and Colombia.

A Vocabulary

A 🎧 **Track 21** Read and listen to the conversation. Notice each word in **blue** and think about its meaning.

Max: Hey, Rika. What's wrong?

Rika: Nothing. I'm just reading the paper.

Max: Well, you're frowning as you read. Facial **expressions** always show your emotions. For example, frowning signals sadness or fear.

Rika: But doesn't that change depending on a person's culture? I'm Indonesian and you're Canadian. We probably just make different facial expressions.

Max: Actually, culture doesn't matter. Back in the 19th century, Charles Darwin found that all people typically make the same facial expressions. He reasoned that these expressions must be a **universal** human characteristic.

Rika: Really? Has anybody else looked into this, or was it just Darwin?

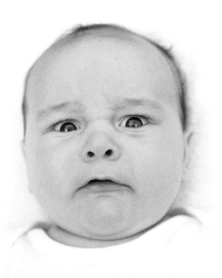

Max: Well, in the 1960s, a psychologist named Paul Ekman confirmed Darwin's theory. He conducted an experiment. He showed photos of facial expressions to people of many different cultures. The **results** showed that people across all cultures recognize—and make—the same facial expressions for the same emotions.

Rika: So culture doesn't matter then, right?

Max: Well, for *some* facial expressions. Neither Darwin nor Ekman could **confirm** that all facial expressions are universal. And Ekman also wondered whether there are things that universally **trigger** certain emotions.

Rika: So, you mean to say that what impacts our emotions is the same for everyone?

Max: Well, yes and no. Certain things are universal. For example, everyone gets scared whenever there's a sudden, unexpected movement in their field of vision.

Rika: That **makes sense**. A sudden movement might signal danger, and there's a **tendency** for humans to **react** to danger. We do it **instinctively**.

Max: Right, but not everything triggers the same emotion in different people. For example, one person might associate the smell of the sea with something enjoyable, like a vacation.

Rika: But for someone who has gotten seasick or been stung by a jellyfish, the ocean isn't so pleasant. So the smell might cause negative emotions.

Max: Exactly! Our reaction is influenced by our experience and, often, our **personality**.

B Discuss the questions with a partner.

1. Are you surprised that facial expressions are the same across cultures? Why or why not?

2. Which emotions do you feel are easiest to recognize? Which are most difficult? Explain.

C Write each word in **blue** from exercise A next to its definition.

1. _____ (n) ways to make your thoughts or feelings known (with gestures, writing, and so on)

2. _____ (v) is logical or easy to understand

3. _____ (n) the outcome

4. _____ (v) to cause a response in someone or something

5. _____ (adv) without having to think

6. _____ (n) a person's character and nature

7. _____ (n) likelihood

8. _____ (adj) experienced by all people

9. _____ (v) to make sure something is right

10. _____ (v) to respond to something or someone

D Complete each question with the correct form of a word from the box.

confirm	expression	instinctively	personality
result	trigger	universal	

1. What _____ fear in you? Joy? Explain.

2. How can you _____ an unbelievable story that you read online?

3. In addition to facial expressions, what else is _____ for humans?

4. What are other forms of _____, besides those that we make with our faces?

5. Think of a time when you tried to make something, but you didn't like the _____. Did you ever try to make it again? Why or why not?

6. If you saw someone in danger, do you think you would _____ try to help that person? Why or why not?

7. How important is _____ in succeeding at a job?

E Discuss the questions from exercise D with a partner. Then use the words below to create three more questions to ask your partner.

make sense	react	tendency

A: *Do your feelings and emotions usually make sense to you?*
B: *Usually, but sometimes I don't understand why I get angry about small things.*

Listening A Lecture about Fear

A skydiver reacts as his instructor behind him opens the parachute.

BEFORE LISTENING

A Before you listen to the lecture, in your notebook make a list of five things that you fear. For each item, note whether you believe this fear is instinctive or whether it is learned.

WHILE LISTENING

LISTENING FOR
MAIN IDEAS

B 🎧 **Track 22** ▶ **3.1** Listen to the lecture. Then choose the best phrase to complete each sentence.

1. The lecture focuses on learning about (our ancestors' fears / the human fear response).

2. It was important for our ancestors to (react instinctively / learn a response) to things like falling rocks and hungry lions.

3. According to the lecture, our fear response can be (useful / dangerous) in certain situations, such as putting on the brakes in a car.

4. In Mineka and Davidson's experiment, the monkeys (were immediately afraid of / learned to fear) snakes.

5. Seeing a video of monkeys being fearful of flowers (impacted / didn't impact) the fear response of the monkeys in the laboratory.

Use a word web to organize your notes as you listen. Write the main topic in the center of the web. Then as you listen, write the words you find essential to the overall message. After listening to the entire passage, go back and write any additional information you need to show how the words connect to the topic.

C 🎧 **Track 22** Listen to the lecture again and write notes in the word web. After you listen, add more details explaining how the ideas connect to fear.

LISTENING FOR DETAILS

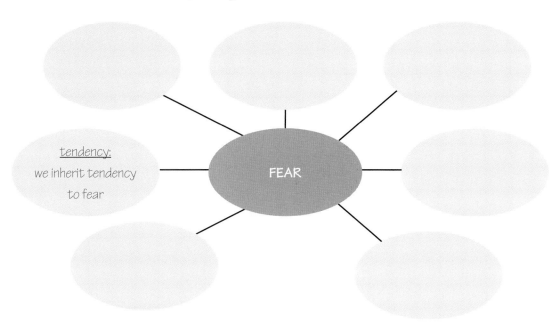

tendency:
we inherit tendency to fear

FEAR

AFTER LISTENING

D Use your word web to complete the sentences with information from the lecture. Then compare your answers with a partner's.

1. The professor discusses _____.

2. The professor shows that some fear is inherited when he talks about _____
   _____.

3. He demonstrates that some fear is learned using the example of _____
   _____.

4. When he talks about the laboratory monkeys' lack of fear of the flowers, the professor is proving that in some cases _____.

E Work in a small group. Discuss these questions.

CRITICAL THINKING: ANALYZING

1. Look back at exercise A. Choose a fear that you identified as learned, and explain how and from whom you may have learned it.

2. Think of something that many people fear, such as flying. Why do you think it causes so much fear? Do you think it is learned or instinctive? Explain.

3. How can you overcome a fear? Explain with examples.

A Speaking

PERSONALIZING **A** Read the summary below. Then discuss the questions with a partner.

HOW DOES THE TEENAGE BRAIN AFFECT BEHAVIOR?

- During the teenage years, an area of the brain called the *prefrontal cortex* is still developing. This part of the brain is essential for decision-making and self-control. Because this part of the brain doesn't mature until adulthood, teenagers typically have weaker reasoning skills and more social anxiety than adults.

- The changes in the brain are evolutionary. They help teens prepare to leave home and go out into the world on their own. The teenage brain is in the process of adapting.

- Parents and teachers often notice the negative behaviors caused by these changes. However, changes in the brain also bring positive behaviors, such as a willingness to try new things and a desire to connect with friends—both necessary skills for adulthood.

1. In general, did you engage in risky behavior as a teen? Why or why not?
2. As a teen, who did you prefer spending time with more—friends or family? Why?
3. According to the information above, was your behavior typical of a teenager, or were you different from the average teen? Explain.

CRITICAL THINKING   Making Judgments

When you make a judgment, you use various pieces of information to analyze a situation. You may combine new information with your own knowledge and previous experiences. For example, you can make a judgment about why an accident happened and support your judgment with reasons.

The driver is distracted while looking at the map on the cell phone.

B Read each situation below. Make judgments about how the teens' brains are affecting their actions. Discuss your ideas in a small group.

CRITICAL THINKING:
MAKING JUDGMENTS

1. Fernando was driving too fast and crashed his father's car into a tree.

2. Lara's teacher asked her to work out a math problem on the board, but she refused. When the teacher asked her again, Lara got angry and walked out of the classroom.

3. Jian spends every evening at his best friend's house, instead of at home with his family. This hurts his mother's feelings.

4. Rachel's volleyball teammates didn't ask her to join them for pizza after the game. Rachel didn't go to volleyball practice the following day.

C Work with a partner. Explain a situation when, as a teenager, you acted in a way that was risky or showed poor judgment. Draw conclusions about what was happening in your brain that may have caused this behavior.

> *Once, I skateboarded down a steep staircase, without a helmet. I knew that it would be fun. I wasn't thinking about the risk, just the reward.*

GRAMMAR FOR SPEAKING *Used To* and *Would*

Use *used to* and *would* followed by a verb to talk about events or situations in the past that happened over a certain period of time, but no longer happen.

Both *used to* and *would* can be used to talk about repeated past actions.
> I **used to** *worry about what other people thought.*
> I **would** *worry about what other people thought.*

Use only *used to* to talk about past states or conditions.
> She **used to** *like watching cartoons on Saturdays.*
> We **used to** *live in Ontario.*
> They **used to** *be best friends.*

In questions and negatives, do not use *-d* on *use to*.
> **Did** *you* **use to** *fight with your sister?*
> *No, I* **didn't use to** *fight with her. We* **used to** *get along well.*

Don't confuse *used to* + verb with *be used to* + noun, which means "familiar with."
> **Are** *you* **used to** *your new neighborhood yet?*

D Complete each question with the correct form of *use to* or *would*. Then answer them with a partner.

1. What TV show _____ like as a child?

2. _____ live someplace other than where you live now? Where?

3. Where _____ go to play with your friends? What

   _____ play?

4. Where _____ go on vacation when you were younger?

5. What class _____ like most in high school? Least?

6. What family member _____ enjoy spending time with most? What

   _____ do together?

E Work with a partner to discuss the topics below. Use *use(d) to* or *would* to talk about being younger. Give examples.

1. take risks
2. fight with family members
3. spend time away from home
4. feel left out
5. your own idea

A: *Did you use to take risks when you were younger?*
B: *Yes, I would take risks. For example, I used to go up on the roof every night.*

PERSONALIZING **F** Think about your life as a child and as a teenager. In the T-chart below, add notes about what you used to do, who you used to spend time with, and what you used to like or dislike. Write at least three things in each column.

As a Child	As a Teenager

EVERYDAY LANGUAGE   Asking Follow-Up Questions

When you're having a conversation, you can use the following expressions to learn more about what the other person is saying.

What is/was that like?   *What do you mean by that?*
Why do you think that is/was?   *What else can you tell me about . . . ?*

G Work with a partner. Using your notes from exercise F, take turns describing yourself both as a child and as a teenager. Use *used to* and *would* in your discussion. When appropriate, use follow-up questions to learn more about your partner.

CRITICAL THINKING: **H** In a small group, discuss the questions.
SYNTHESIZING

1. How did your behavior change in your teenage years? How does this compare with other members of the group?
2. What stayed the same between your childhood and teenage years? Explain.
3. How can researchers use information about the teenage brain to help parents and teachers better understand and relate to teenagers?

LESSON TASK Presenting Survey Results

A Follow these steps. Take notes in the chart below.

1. Choose a negative emotion to ask about and complete the questions.
2. Add one more question about this emotion.
3. Ask a classmate the questions and take notes on the answers.
4. Repeat with two more classmates.

Survey Questions	Name: _____	Name: _____	Name: _____
1. How often do you feel _____? (i.e., once a day, several times a week.)			
2. What triggers _____ in you?			
3. How do you show that you feel _____? (i.e., facial expressions, certain behaviors.)			
4. What behavior related to this emotion do you think you have learned?			
5. _____ _____			

B Use your survey results to prepare a short summary. In your summary you will describe common triggers of the emotion as well as how people respond to it, without giving names.

C Form a small group with two or three classmates that you did *not* interview in your survey. Present what you learned about the classmates that you surveyed, without providing personal details or names. Then listen as group members share their results. Ask follow-up questions to learn more.

PRESENTING

> *The emotion that I asked about in my survey was jealousy. Many people felt it every day . . .*

Video

Cory Richards photographed himself moments after an avalanche on Gasherbrum II in the Himalayas on the border of Pakistan and China.

Discomfort

BEFORE VIEWING

A Work with a partner. Discuss the meaning of some words you will hear in the video. Use a dictionary if needed. Then categorize the words as generally positive (+) or negative (–). Some words can go in either category.

adventure (n)	experience (n)	triumph (v)
avalanche (n)	hurt (v)	unknown (adj)
comfortable (adj)	stress (n)	
confusing (adj)	struggle (n)	

B Read the information about Cory Richards. What kind of person do you think he is? What adjectives would you use to describe him? List four adjectives.

_____

> **MEET CORY RICHARDS.** Mountain climber, photojournalist, and visual storyteller, National Geographic Photographer Cory Richards has traveled from the peaks of Antarctica to the Himalayas to capture the soul of adventure and the beauty of our world. He was named 2012 National Geographic Adventurer of the Year. He is one of the world's leading adventure photographers.

WHILE VIEWING

C ▶ 3.2 Watch the video and choose the best answers.

UNDERSTANDING
MAIN IDEAS

1. For Richards, photography is a way to _____.
   a. communicate what it means to be human
   b. document incredible and dangerous adventures
   c. share beautiful images from around the world

2. Richards is motivated to _____.
   a. photograph world problems and issues
   b. go to the highest peaks in the world
   c. explore what is unknown to him

3. The purpose of this video is _____.
   a. to inspire others to climb mountains
   b. to explain what motivates him to take photographs
   c. to tell the story of his life

D ▶ 3.2 Watch the video again. Complete the sentences with the words you hear.

UNDERSTANDING
DETAILS

1. I think _____ is anything that puts us outside our comfort zone.

2. When I _____ that I had not died, I turned the camera on myself and took an image.

3. I've never been _____ in the place that I'm in. I can't stop and sit.

4. I've seen faces that are just years and years of history all wrapped into one single _____ .

5. My job is to communicate a _____ , raw, visceral[1] experience.

6. I mean, life is _____ .

7. This started as a way for me to communicate what I was _____ .

[1] **visceral** (adj): deeply felt feelings that are difficult to control

AFTER VIEWING

E In a small group, discuss the questions below.

CRITICAL THINKING:
ANALYZING

1. Read statements 1, 3, and 6 in exercise D. Are any of them true for you? How would you change any statements to make them true for you?
2. Look at how you categorized the words in exercise A. How do you think Cory Richards would categorize them? Discuss and explain your reasons.
3. Think about the title of the video: A Tribute to Discomfort. A tribute shows admiration or respect for something or someone. In what way might Richards respect or admire discomfort? What is your attitude toward discomfort?
4. Have you (or someone you know) had an experience that changed your life? Describe it.

EMOTIONS AND PERSONALITY **53**

B Vocabulary

A Make a list of words to describe your personality (e.g., curious, shy, agreeable).

_____   _____   _____

_____   _____   _____

MEANING FROM CONTEXT **B** 🎧 **Track 23** Read and listen to the information. Notice each word in **blue** and think about its meaning.

INTROVERT AND EXTROVERT

Modern psychology offers many models to explain personality types, but nearly all of them include two terms made popular by Carl Jung in the early 20th century: **introvert** and **extrovert**. These two personality types have very different characteristics, and while almost everyone has some aspects of both in their own personality, one type is usually stronger.

In general, introverts prefer activities they can do alone, such as reading or playing video games. For most people, being an introvert simply means preferring less frequent social contact with smaller numbers of people—going out with friends one-on-one, instead of in a large group, for example. In more extreme cases, introverts may feel **awkward** in social situations and may even feel so much **anxiety** that they avoid socializing altogether.

Extroverts **differ** from introverts in several ways. Extroverts **thrive** on interaction with others and feel energized at big social gatherings. They often have jobs in which they collaborate with others—teachers and politicians tend to be extroverts, for example. While people often find extroverts charming, some can be too talkative and **outgoing**, to the point that others may feel uncomfortable around them. Extroverts often become **upset** when they **lack** human contact on the job or in their social lives. Sometimes feelings of being alone can even **lead to** depression. In general, extroverts tend to feel best about themselves in the company of others.

C Look at the words you wrote to describe yourself in exercise A. Are you more of an introvert, extrovert, or a combination? Discuss with a partner.

D Write each word in **blue** from exercise B next to its definition.

1. _____ (adj) unhappy or disappointed
2. _____ (v) to vary, be different from
3. _____ (v ph) to result in
4. _____ (n) a feeling of extreme nervousness or worry
5. _____ (v) to have too little of
6. _____ (n) a person who prefers to spend time alone or in small groups
7. _____ (adj) friendly, enjoys meeting others
8. _____ (v) to be motivated, energized by
9. _____ (n) a person who prefers to spend time with other people
10. _____ (adj) uncomfortable and embarrassed

VOCABULARY SKILL Identifying Latin Prefixes and Suffixes

Many words in English take prefixes and suffixes that originate from Latin. Here are some Latin prefixes and suffixes commonly used in English.

Prefix	Meaning	Suffix	Meaning
co-	*together*	-able, -ible	*capable, able to*
inter-	*between, among*	-er, -or	*one who (does something)*
intro-	*inward*	-ion, -sion, -tion	*act of, result of*
pre-	*before*	-ive	*having a tendency to*
re-	*again*	-logy	*the study of*

E Notice the prefix and/or suffix in each word. Then write another word with that same word part. Use a dictionary if necessary.

1. introverted *introspective*
2. depression _____
3. talkative _____
4. psychology _____
5. comfortable _____
6. teacher _____
7. collaborate _____
8. interaction _____
9. preteen _____
10. reconfirm _____

F Work with a partner. Discuss these questions.

1. Describe someone you know who is very outgoing. What are some other personality characteristics of the person?
2. Describe situations in which people often feel awkward. Explain why they may feel that way.
3. Why do people suffer from anxiety in today's world? Give at least three reasons.

Listening A Conversation about Food and Emotions

BEFORE LISTENING

PERSONALIZING **A** You are going to hear a conversation about how eating is connected with personality and emotions. How do your emotions affect what you eat? Does what you eat affect your emotions? Write your ideas. Then discuss them with a partner.

WHILE LISTENING

LISTENING SKILL Listening for Consequences

It is important to understand the relationship between actions and the consequences (results). Here are some words and phrases that often signal consequences.

if clauses
> *If you get more exercise, you will sleep better at night.*

when clauses
> *When I sleep well, I wake up in a good mood the next day.*

because clauses
> *She got lost because she wasn't paying attention.*

lead to
> *Long-term job stress can lead to health problems.*

B 🎧 **Track 24** Complete each statement with your own idea of a consequence. Then listen to find out what the person actually says. Were your consequences different?

1. I have a tendency to _____ when I'm stressed.

2. If you eat healthy foods today, you'll _____.

3. If you're in a good mood, you'll feel more _____.

4. Diets that contain a lot of sugar can lead to _____.

5. Extroverts eat _____ because they're always socializing.

LISTENING FOR **C** 🎧 **Track 25** Listen to the first part of the conversation. Write answers to the questions
MAIN IDEAS in your notebook. Then compare with a partner.

1. How does Sam feel? Why?

_____

2. Why does Mae want him to throw out his snack?

_____

3. What does Mae say about eating unhealthy food?

_____

4. How does Sam react to Mae's suggestions?

_____

D 🎧 **Track 26** Listen to the second part of the conversation. Mark the statements T for *True* or F for *False*. Correct the false statements.

LISTENING FOR DETAILS

1. Foods you eat can affect how you feel a few days later.　　　T　　　F

2. Your personality has nothing to do with your diet.　　　T　　　F

3. Extroverts have a tendency to be healthy eaters.　　　T　　　F

4. In some cases, picky eating can be a sign of anxiety.　　　T　　　F

AFTER LISTENING

E 🎧 **Track 27** Listen to each person talk about his or her emotions. Then write the letter of the food that each person might eat based on what you hear. Compare your answers with a partner. Explain the inferences you made for each.

CRITICAL THINKING: MAKING INFERENCES

1. _____　　2. _____　　3. _____　　4. _____

a.

b.

c.

d.

F Work in a small group. Discuss the questions.

CRITICAL THINKING: EVALUATING

1. Look at your responses for exercise A. Did the new information change your ideas about the relationship between eating and emotions for you? Explain.

2. What unusual eating habits do you have? For example, do you eat all of one type of food before starting another? Do you eat special kinds of food? Are you willing to try really unusual foods? What do you think these habits say about your personality?

3. What else affects how and what you eat? What can you change to be healthier? How might those changes, in turn, affect your personality?

B Speaking

A Discuss the questions in small groups.

1. Look back at your list of personality traits from the vocabulary section of this lesson. How many of these attributes are positive? Negative?
2. If you could change one thing about your personality, what would it be? Why?

CRITICAL THINKING:
APPLYING

B 🎧 **Track 28** Look at the graphic and listen to the description. Then read the description of each person below. Identify which of the Big 5 aspects each person is most associated with and discuss your answers with a partner.

The Big 5 Personality Aspects

1. Lisa is working toward a promotion at her job. She comes early and stays late every day, and her boss knows that he can depend on Lisa to get the job done.
2. Daigo is so popular! It feels like everyone on campus knows him. I don't know how he does it.
3. Hector is hard to be around. He seems annoyed by everything I say! He always seems nervous or stressed about something.
4. Ana just signed up for a course on acrobatics! And last year, she learned to go deep-sea fishing. She is always doing something unusual.
5. Giselle is a very generous person. She's always doing volunteer work in the community. Her neighbors' well-being is really important to her.

CRITICAL THINKING:
JUDGING

C Look at the graphic in exercise B. Rate your personality (or that of a family member) for each of the five aspects. Rate 1 for *not very* up to 5 for *very*.

_____ Openness   _____ Agreeableness

_____ Dependability   _____ Neuroticism

_____ Extroversion

D With a partner, give examples of behavior that demonstrate your ratings in exercise C.

> *I really like trying new things! For example, last week, I went skydiving. I must be strong in the "openness" category. Maybe I'm a 5?*

PRONUNCIATION Using Punctuation Marks

When you're reading aloud, use the punctuation marks to guide how you pronounce sentences. When you see:

. → use falling intonation

, / ; / : / . . . → pause

? → use rising or falling intonation to show a question

! → use stress to show emphasis

" " → add emphasis to that word

E With a partner, read the conversation model in exercise D aloud, focusing on the correct pronunciation for each punctuation mark. Then write down one of the answers that you gave in exercise D and read it aloud.

F 🎧 **Track 29** Listen to the conversation about changing your personality. Then discuss the questions with a partner.

1. In a research study, what percent of people were satisfied with their personality? Are you surprised at this number? Explain.
2. What do Luis and Alma want to change about their personalities?
3. According to the article Alma read, how can you change your personality?

SPEAKING SKILL Defending an Opinion

When you give your opinion, you should provide facts to make your argument stronger. Use the phrases below to introduce facts to defend your opinion.

I read that *the teenage brain is less developed than the adult brain.*

Most people would agree that *extroverted people are fun to be around.*

As far as I know, *fear is a learned behavior.*

Research suggests that *personality can change over time.*

G In exercise F, you heard about how personality changes. Give your opinion of how the life events below can change you and defend your opinion.

CRITICAL THINKING: ANALYZING

1. getting a job that you really like
2. having a baby
3. getting married
4. moving to a new place

FINAL TASK Presenting Research

> You and a partner are going to research one of the topics below and prepare an interactive presentation on the topic for the class:
>
> - the effects of sleep on the brain
> - how different genders show the same emotions
> - the relationship between personality type and exercise
> - behavior and emotions in young children

PRESENTATION SKILL Interacting with the Audience

When giving a presentation, try to engage your audience. You can do this in any of the following ways:

- Ask audience members what they already know about the topic.
- Ask for volunteers to share personal stories that relate to your topic.
- Hold a question-and-answer session at the end of your presentation.

Here are three important tips:

- After someone participates, follow up by relating what he or she said directly to your topic.
- Don't hesitate to politely interrupt an audience member if what he or she is saying is off topic.
- Only call on a person who volunteers to answer.

A Work with a partner. Select one of the topics above to research. Before you begin researching, write five questions that you want to answer in your research.

ORGANIZING IDEAS **B** With your partner, compile your research into a presentation. Organize the subtopics according to the five questions you wrote in exercise A. Then for one or two of the subtopics, write a relevant question for the audience.

PRESENTING **C** With your partner, give your presentation. Take turns engaging your audience and responding to their input.

REFLECTION

1. What information about psychology are you most likely to remember? Why?

_____

_____

2. What is the most useful thing you learned in this unit?

_____

_____

3. Here are the vocabulary words from the unit. Check (✓) the ones you can use.

☐ anxiety	☐ introvert	☐ result
☐ awkward	☐ lack	☐ tendency
☐ confirm **AWL**	☐ lead to	☐ thrive
☐ differ	☐ make sense	☐ trigger **AWL**
☐ expression	☐ outgoing	☐ universal
☐ extrovert	☐ personality	☐ upset
☐ instinctively	☐ react **AWL**	

Independent Student Handbook

LISTENING SKILLS

Predicting

Speakers giving formal talks usually begin by introducing themselves and their topic. Listen carefully to the introduction of the topic so that you can predict what the talk will be about.

Strategies:

- Use visual information including titles on the board or on presentation slides.
- Think about what you already know about the topic.
- Ask yourself questions that you think the speaker might answer.
- Listen for specific phrases that indicate an introduction (e.g., *My topic is…*).

Listening for Main Ideas

It is important to be able to tell the difference between a speaker's main ideas and supporting details. It is more common for teachers to test understanding of main ideas than of specific details.

Strategies:

- Listen carefully to the introduction. Speakers often state the main idea in the introduction.
- Listen for rhetorical questions, or questions that the speaker asks, and then answers. Often the answer is the statement of the main idea.
- Notice words and phrases that the speaker repeats. Repetition often signals main ideas.

Listening for Details (Examples)

A speaker often provides examples that support a main idea. A good example can help you understand and remember the main idea better.

Strategies:

- Listen for specific phrases that introduce examples.
- Listen for general statements. Examples often follow general statements.

Listening for Details (Cause and Effect)

Speakers often give reasons or list causes and/or effects to support their ideas.

Strategies:

- Notice nouns that might signal causes/reasons (e.g., *factors, influences, causes, reasons*) or effects/results (e.g., *effects, results, outcomes, consequences*).
- Notice verbs that might signal causes/reasons (e.g., *contribute to, affect, influence, determine, produce, result in*) or effects/results (often these are passive, e.g., *is affected by*).

Understanding the Structure of a Presentation

An organized speaker uses expressions to alert the audience to important information that will follow. Recognizing signal words and phrases will help you understand how a presentation is organized and the relationship between ideas.

Introduction

A good introduction identifies the topic and gives an idea of how the lecture or presentation will be organized. Here are some expressions to introduce a topic:

I'll be talking about . . .	*My topic is . . .*
There are basically two groups . . .	*There are three reasons . . .*

Body

In the body of a lecture, speakers usually expand upon the topic. They often use phrases that signal the order of events or subtopics and their relationship to each other. Here are some expressions to help listeners follow the body of a lecture:

The first/next/final (point/reason) is . . .	*First/Next/Finally, let's look at . . .*
Another reason is . . .	*However, . . .*

Conclusion

In the conclusion of a lecture, speakers often summarize what they have said. They may also make predictions or suggestions. Sometimes they ask a question in the conclusion to get the audience to think more about the topic. Here are some expressions to give a conclusion:

In conclusion, . . .	*In summary, . . .*
As you can see. . .	*To review, + (restatement of main points)*

Understanding Meaning from Context

When you are not familiar with a word that a speaker says, you can sometimes guess the meaning of the word or fill in the gaps using the context or situation itself.

Strategies:

- Don't panic. You don't always understand every word of what a speaker says in your first language, either.
- Use context clues to fill in the blanks. What did you understand just before or just after the missing part? What did the speaker probably say?
- Listen for words and phrases that signal a definition or explanation (e.g., *What that means is . . .*).

Recognizing a Speaker's Bias

Speakers often have an opinion about the topic they are discussing. It's important for you to know if they are objective or subjective about the topic. Objective speakers do not express an opinion. Subjective speakers have a bias or a strong feeling about the topic.

Strategies:

- Notice words like adjectives, adverbs, and modals that the speaker uses (e.g., *ideal, horribly, should, shouldn't*). These suggest that the speaker has a bias.
- Listen to the speaker's voice. Does he or she sound excited, angry, or bored?
- Notice if the speaker gives more weight or attention to one point of view over another.
- Listen for words that signal opinions (e.g., *I think…*).

NOTE-TAKING SKILLS

Taking notes is a personalized skill. It is important to develop a note-taking system that works for you. However, there are some common strategies to improve your note taking.

Before You Listen

Focus

Try to clear your mind before the speaker begins so you can pay attention. If possible, review previous notes or think about what you already know about the topic.

Predict

If you know the topic of the talk, think about what you might hear.

Listen

Take Notes by Hand

Research suggests that taking notes by hand rather than on a computer is more effective. Taking notes by hand requires you to summarize, rephrase, and synthesize information. This helps you *encode* the information, or put it into a form that you can understand and remember.

Listen for Signal Words and Phrases

Speakers often use signal words and phrases (e.g., *Today we're going to talk about…*) to organize their ideas and show relationships between them. Listening for signal words and phrases can help you decide what information to write in your notes.

Condense (Shorten) Information

- As you listen, focus on the most important ideas. The speaker will usually repeat, define, explain, and/or give examples of these ideas. Take notes on these ideas.

    Speaker: *The Itaipu Dam provides about 20% of the electricity used in Brazil and about 75% of the electricity used in Paraguay. That electricity goes to millions of homes and businesses, so it's good for the economy of both countries.*

    Notes: Itaipu Dam → electricity: Brazil 20%, Paraguay 75%

- Don't write full sentences. Write only key words (nouns, verbs, adjectives, and adverbs), phrases, or short sentences.

    Full sentence: *Teachers are normally at the top of the list of happiest jobs.*

    Notes: teachers happiest

- Leave out information that is obvious.

> Full sentence: *Photographer Annie Griffiths is famous for her beautiful photographs. She travels all over the world to take photos.*
>
> Notes: A. *Griffiths famous for photos; travels world*

- Write numbers and statistics using numerals (9 bil; 35%).
- Use abbreviations (e.g., *ft., min., yr*) and symbols (=, ≠, >, <, %, →).
- Use indenting. Write main ideas on the left side of the paper. Indent details.

> *Benefits of eating ugly foods*
>> *Save $*
>>> *10-20% on ugly fruits & vegs. at market*

- Write details under key terms to help you remember them.
- Write the definitions of important new words.

After You Listen

- Review your notes soon after the lecture or presentation. Add any details you missed.
- Clarify anything you don't understand in your notes with a classmate or teacher.
- Add or highlight main ideas. Cross out details that aren't important or necessary.
- Rewrite anything that is hard to read or understand. Rewrite your notes in an outline or other graphic organizer to organize the information more clearly.
- Use arrows, boxes, diagrams, or other visual cues to show relationships between ideas.

ORGANIZING INFORMATION

You can use a graphic organizer to take notes while you are listening, or to organize your notes after you listen. Here are some examples of graphic organizers:

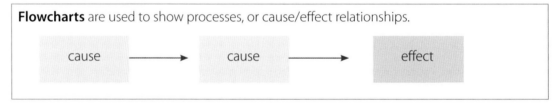

Flowcharts are used to show processes, or cause/effect relationships.

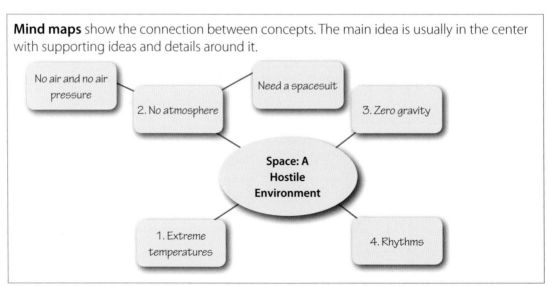

Mind maps show the connection between concepts. The main idea is usually in the center with supporting ideas and details around it.

Outlines show the relationship between main ideas and details.

To use an outline for taking notes, write the main ideas at the left margin of your paper. Below the main ideas, indent and write the supporting ideas and details. You may do this as you listen, or go back and rewrite your notes as an outline later.

> **I. Introduction:** How to feed the world
>
> **II. Steps**
>
>   Step One: Stop deforestation
>
>   a. stop burning rainforests
>
>   b. grow crops on land size of South America

T-charts compare two topics.

Climate Change in Greenland	
Benefits	**Drawbacks**
shorter winters	rising sea levels

Timelines show a sequence of events.

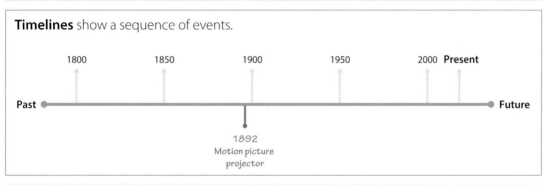

1800   1850   1900   1950   2000 **Present**

Past — Future

1892
Motion picture
projector

Venn diagrams compare and contrast two or more topics. The overlapping areas show similarities.

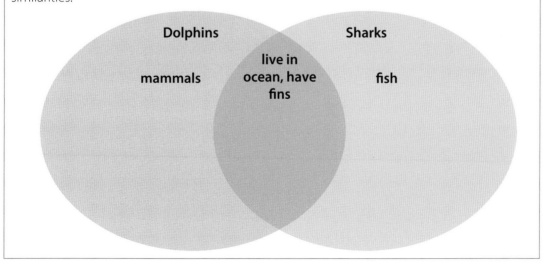

Dolphins   Sharks

mammals   live in ocean, have fins   fish

SPEAKING: COMMON PHRASES

Phrases for Expressing Yourself

Expressing Opinions
I think…
I believe…
I'm sure…
In my opinion/view…
If you ask me,…
Personally,…
To me,…

Expressing Likes and Dislikes
I like…
I prefer…
I love…
I can't stand…
I hate…
I really don't like…
I don't care for…

Giving Facts
There is evidence/proof…
Experts claim/argue…
Studies show…
Researchers found…
The record shows…

Giving Tips or Suggestions
Imperatives (e.g., Try to get more sleep.)
You/We should/shouldn't…
You/We ought to…
It's (not) a good idea to…
I suggest (that)…
Let's…
How about… + (noun/gerund)
What about… + (noun/gerund)
Why don't we/you…
You/We could…

Agreeing
I agree.
True.
Good point.
Exactly.
Absolutely.
I was just about to say that.
Definitely.
Right!

Disagreeing
I disagree.
I'm not so sure about that.
I don't know.
That's a good point, but I don't agree.
I see what you mean, but I think that…

Phrases for Interacting with Others

Clarifying/Checking Your Understanding

So are you saying that…?
So what you mean is…?
What do you mean?
How's that?
How so?
I'm not sure I understand/follow.
Do you mean…?
I'm not sure what you mean.

Asking for Clarification/Confirming Understanding

Sorry, I didn't catch that. Could you repeat it?
I'm not sure I understand the question.
I'm not sure I understand what you mean.
Sorry, I'm not following you.
Are you saying that…?
If I understand correctly, you're saying that…
Oh, now I get it. You're talking about…, right?

Checking Others' Understanding

Does that make sense?
Do you understand?
Do you see what I mean?
Is that clear?
Are you following/with me?
Do you have any questions?

Asking for Opinions

What do you think?
We haven't heard from you in a while.
Do you have anything to add?
What are your thoughts?
How do you feel?
What's your opinion?

Taking Turns

Can/May I say something?
Could I add something?
Can I just say…?
May I continue?
Can I finish what I was saying?
Did you finish your thought?
Let me finish.
Let's get back to…

Interrupting Politely

Excuse me.
Pardon me.
Forgive me for interrupting…
I hate to interrupt but…
Can I stop you for a second?

Asking for Repetition

Could you say that again?
I'm sorry?
I didn't catch what you said.
I'm sorry. I missed that. What did you say?
Could you repeat that please?

Showing Interest

I see.	*Good for you.*
Really?	*Seriously?*
Um-hmm.	*No kidding!*
Wow.	*And? (Then what?)*

That's funny / amazing / incredible / awful!

SPEAKING: PHRASES FOR PRESENTING

Introduction

Introducing a Topic

I'm going to talk about…
My topic is…
I'm going to present…
I plan to discuss…
Let's start with…

Today we're going to talk about…
So we're going to show you…
Now/Right/So/Well, (pause), let's look at…
There are three groups/reasons/effects/factors…
There are four steps in this process.

Body

Listing or Sequencing

First/First of all/The first (noun)/To start/To begin,…
Second/Secondly/The second/Next/Another/Also/Then/In addition,…
Last/The last/Finally,…
There are many/several/three types/kinds of/ways…

Signaling Problems/Solutions

One problem/issue/challenge is…
One solution/answer/response is…

Giving Reasons or Causes

Because + (clause): Because the climate is changing…
Because of + (noun phrase): Because of climate change…
Due to + (noun phrase)…
Since + (clause)
The reason that I like hip-hop is…
One reason that people listen to music is…
One factor is + (noun phrase)
The main reason that…

Giving Results or Effects

so + (clause): so I went to the symphony
Therefore, + (sentence): Therefore, I went to the symphony.
As a result, + (sentence)
Consequently, + (sentence)
…causes + (noun phrase)
…leads to + (noun phrase)
…had an impact/effect on + (noun phrase)
If…then…

Giving Examples

The first example is…
Here's an example of what I mean…
For instance,…
For example,…
Let me give you an example…
…such as…
…like…

Repeating and Rephrasing

What you need to know is…
I'll say this again…
So again, let me repeat…
The most important point is…

Signaling Additional Examples or Ideas	Signaling to Stop Taking Notes
Not only…, but	*You don't need this for the test.*
Besides…	*This information is in your books/on your handout/on the website.*
Not only do…, but also	*You don't have to write all this down.*

Identifying a Side Track	Returning to a Previous Topic
This is off-topic,…	*Getting back to our previous discussion,…*
On a different subject,…	*To return to our earlier topic…*
As an aside, …	*OK, getting back on topic…*
That reminds me…	*So to return to what we were saying,…*

Signaling a Definition	Talking about Visuals
Which means…	*This graph/infographic/diagram shows/explains…*
What that means is…	*The line/box/image represents…*
Or…	*The main point of this visual is…*
In other words,…	*You can see…*
Another way to say that is…	*From this we can see…*
That is…	
That is to say…	

Conclusion

Concluding	
Well/So, that's how I see it.	*To sum up,*
In conclusion,	*As you can see,…*
In summary,	*At the end,…*
	To review, (+ restatement of main points)

PRESENTATION STRATEGIES

You will often have to give individual or group presentations in your class. The strategies below will help you to prepare, present, and reflect on your presentations.

Prepare

As you prepare your presentation:

Consider Your Topic

- **Choose a topic you feel passionate about.** If you are passionate about your topic, your audience will be more interested and excited about your topic, too. Focus on one major idea that you can bring to life. The best ideas are the ones your audience wants to experience.

Consider Your Purpose

- **Have a strong start.** Use an effective hook, such as a quote, an interesting example, a rhetorical question, or a powerful image to get your audience's attention. Include one sentence that explains what you will do in your presentation and why.
- **Stay focused.** Make sure your details and examples support your main points. Avoid sidetracks or unnecessary information that takes you away from your topic.
- **Use visuals that relate to your ideas.** Drawings, photos, video clips, infographics, charts, maps, slides, and physical objects can get your audience's attention and explain ideas effectively. For example, a photo or map of a location you mention can help your audience picture a place they have never been. Slides with only key words and phrases can help emphasize your main points. Visuals should be bright, clear, and simple.
- **Have a strong conclusion.** A strong conclusion should serve the same purpose as a strong start—to get your audience's attention and make them think. Good conclusions often refer back to the introduction, or beginning of the presentation. For example, if you ask a question in the beginning, you can answer it in the conclusion. Remember to restate your main points, and add a conclusion device such as a question, a call to action, or a quote.

Consider Your Audience

- **Use familiar concepts.** Think about the people in your audience. Ask yourself these questions: Where are they from? How old are they? What is their background? What do they already know about my topic? What information do I need to explain? Use language and concepts they will understand.
- **Share a personal story.** Consider presenting information that will get an emotional reaction; for example, information that will make your audience feel surprised, curious, worried, or upset. This will help your audience relate to you and your topic.
- **Be authentic (be yourself!).** Write your presentation yourself. Use words that you know and are comfortable using.

Rehearse

- **Make an outline** to help you organize your ideas.
- **Write notes on notecards.** Do not write full sentences, just key words and phrases to help you remember important ideas. Mark the words you should stress and places to pause.
- **Review pronunciation.** Check the pronunciation of words you are uncertain about with a classmate, a teacher, or in a dictionary. Note and practice the pronunciation of difficult words.
- **Memorize the introduction and conclusion.** Rehearse your presentation several times. Practice saying it out loud to yourself (perhaps in front of a mirror or video recorder) and in front of others.
- **Ask for feedback.** Note and revise information that doesn't flow smoothly based on feedback and on your own performance in rehearsal. If specific words or phrases are still a problem, rephrase them.

Present

As you present:

- **Pay attention to your pacing** (how fast or slow you speak). Remember to speak slowly and clearly. Pause to allow your audience to process information.
- **Speak at a volume loud enough to be heard** by everyone in the audience, but not too loud. Ask the audience if your volume is OK at the beginning of your talk.

- **Vary your intonation.** Don't speak in the same tone throughout the talk. Your audience will be more interested if your voice rises and falls, speeds up and slows down to match the ideas you are talking about.
- **Be friendly and relaxed with your audience**—remember to smile!
- **Show enthusiasm for your topic.** Use humor if appropriate.
- **Have a relaxed body posture.** Don't stand with your arms folded, or look down at your notes. Use gestures when helpful to emphasize your points.
- **Don't read directly from your notes.** Use them to help you remember ideas.
- **Don't look at or read from your visuals too much.** Use them to support your ideas.
- **Make frequent eye contact** with the entire audience.

Reflect

As you reflect on your presentation:

- **Consider what you think went well** during your presentation and what areas you can improve upon.
- **Get feedback** from your classmates and teacher. How do their comments relate to your own thoughts about your presentation? Did they notice things you didn't? How can you use their feedback in your next presentation?

PRESENTATION OUTLINE

When you are planning a presentation, you may find it helpful to use an outline. If it is a group presentation, the outline can provide an easy way to divide the content. For example, one student can do the introduction, another student the first idea in the body, and so on.

1. Introduction

Topic: _____

Hook: _____

Statement of main idea: _____

2. Body

First step/example/reason: _____

    Supporting details: _____ _____ _____

Second step/example/reason: _____

    Supporting details: _____ _____ _____

Third step/example/reason: _____

    Supporting details: _____ _____ _____

3. Conclusion

Main points to summarize: _____ _____

Suggestions/Predictions: _____ _____

Closing comments/summary: _____ _____

PRONUNCIATION GUIDE

Sounds and Symbols

Vowels

Symbol	Key Words
/ɑ/	hot, stop
/æ/	cat, ran
/aɪ/	fine, nice
/i/	eat, need
/ɪ/	sit, him
/eɪ/	name, say
/ɛ/	get, bed
/ʌ/	cup, what
/ə/	about, lesson
/u/	boot, new
/ʊ/	book, could
/oʊ/	go, road
/ɔ/	law, walk
/aʊ/	house, now
/ɔɪ/	toy, coin

Consonants

Symbol	Key Word	Symbol	Key Word
/b/	boy	/t/	tea
/d/	day	/tʃ/	cheap
/dʒ/	job, bridge	/v/	vote
/f/	face	/w/	we
/g/	go	/y/	yes
/h/	hat	/z/	zoo
/k/	key, car		
/l/	love	/ð/	they
/m/	my	/θ/	think
/n/	nine	/ʃ/	shoe
/ŋ/	sing	/ʒ/	measure
/p/	pen		
/r/	right		
/s/	see		

Source: *The Newbury House Dictionary plus Grammar Reference*, Fifth Edition, National Geographic Learning/ Cengage Learning, 2014.

Rhythm

The rhythm of English involves stress and pausing.

Stress

- English words are based on syllables—units of sound that include one vowel sound.
- In every word in English, one syllable has the primary stress.
- In English, speakers group words that go together based on the meaning and context of the sentence. These groups of words are called *thought groups*. In each thought group, one word is stressed more than the others—the stress is placed on the syllable with the primary stress in this word.
- In general, new ideas and information are stressed.

Pausing

- Pauses in English can be divided into two groups: long and short pauses.
- English speakers use long pauses to mark the conclusion of a thought, items in a list, or choices given.
- Short pauses are used in between thought groups to break up the ideas in sentences into smaller, more manageable chunks of information.

English speakers use intonation, or pitch (the rise and fall of their voice), to help express meaning. For example, speakers usually use a rising intonation at the end of *yes/no* questions, and a falling intonation at the end of *wh-* questions and statements.

VOCABULARY BUILDING STRATEGIES

Vocabulary learning is an on-going process. The strategies below will help you learn and remember new vocabulary words.

Guessing Meaning from Context

You can often guess the meaning of an unfamiliar word by looking at or listening to the words and sentences around it. Speakers usually know when a word is unfamiliar to the audience, or is essential to understanding the main ideas, and often provide clues to its meaning.

- Repetition: A speaker may use the same key word or phrase, or use another form of the same word.
- Restatement or synonym: A speaker may give a synonym to explain the meaning of a word, using phrases such as *in other words, also called, or…, also known as*.
- Antonyms: A speaker may define a word by explaining what it is NOT. The speaker may say *Unlike A/In contrast to A, B is…*
- Definition: Listen for signals such as *which means* or *is defined as*. Definitions can also be signaled by a pause.
- Examples: A speaker may provide examples that can help you figure out what something is. For example, **Mascots** *are a very popular marketing tool. You've seen them on commercials and in ads on social media –* **cute, brightly colored creatures that help sell a product**.

Understanding Word Families: Stems, Prefixes, and Suffixes

Use your understanding of stems, prefixes, and suffixes to recognize unfamiliar words and to expand your vocabulary. The stem is the root part of the word, which provides the main meaning. A prefix comes before the stem and usually modifies meaning (e.g., adding *re-* to a word means "again" or "back"). A suffix comes after the stem and usually changes the part of speech (e.g., adding *-ion, -tion,* or *-ation* to a verb changes it to a noun). Words that share the same stem or root belong to the same word family (e.g., *event, eventful, uneventful, uneventfully*).

Word Stem	Meaning	Example
ann, enn	year	anniversary, millennium
chron(o)	time	chronological, synchronize
flex, flect	bend	flexible, reflection
graph	draw, write	graphics, paragraph
lab	work	labor, collaborate
mob, mot, mov	move	automobile, motivate, mover
port	carry	transport, import
sect	cut	sector, bisect

Prefix	Meaning	Example
dis-	not, opposite of	disappear, disadvantages
in-, im-, il-, ir-	not	inconsistent, immature, illegal, irresponsible
inter-	between	Internet, international
mis-	bad, badly, incorrectly	misunderstand, misjudge
pre-	before	prehistoric, preheat
re-	again; back	repeat; return
trans-	across, beyond	transfer, translate
un-	not	uncooked, unfair

Suffix	Meaning	Example
-able, -ible	worth, ability	believable, impossible
-en	to cause to become; made of	lengthen, strengthen; golden
-er, -or	one who	teacher, director
-ful	full of	beautiful, successful
-ify, -fy	to make or become	simplify, satisfy
-ion, -tion, -ation	condition, action	occasion, education, foundation
-ize	cause	modernize, summarize
-ly	in the manner of	carefully, happily
-ment	condition or result	assignment, statement
-ness	state of being	happiness, sadness

Using a Dictionary

Here are some tips for using a dictionary:

- When you see or hear a new word, try to guess its part of speech (noun, verb, adjective, etc.) and meaning, then look it up in a dictionary.

- Some words have multiple meanings. Look up a new word in the dictionary and try to choose the correct meaning for the context. Then see if it makes sense within the context.

- When you look up a word, look at all the definitions to see if there is a basic core meaning. This will help you understand the word when it is used in a different context. Also look at all the related words, or words in the same family. This can help you expand your vocabulary. For example, the core meaning of *structure* involves something built or put together.

> **structure** / ˈstrʌktʃər/ *n.* **1** [C] a building of any kind: *A new structure is being built on the corner.* **2** [C] any architectural object of any kind: *The Eiffel Tower is a famous Parisian structure.* **3** [U] the way parts are put together or organized: *the structure of a song‖a business's structure*
> *–v.* [T] **-tured, -turing, -tures** to put together or organize parts of s.t.: *We are structuring a plan to hire new teachers.*
> *-adj.* **structural.**

Source: *The Newbury House Dictionary plus Grammar Reference*, Fifth Edition, National Geographic Learning/Cengage Learning, 2014

Multi-Word Units

You can improve your fluency if you learn and use vocabulary as multi-word units: idioms (*go the extra mile*), collocations (*wide range*), and fixed expressions (*in other words*). Some multi-word units can only be understood as a chunk—the individual words do not add up to the same overall meaning. Keep track of multi-word units in a notebook or on notecards.

Vocabulary Note Cards

You can expand your vocabulary by using vocabulary note cards or a vocabulary building app. Write the word, expression, or sentence that you want to learn on one side. On the other, draw a four-square grid and write the following information in the squares: definition; translation (in your first language); sample sentence; synonyms. Choose words that are high frequency or on the academic word list. If you have looked a word up a few times, you should make a card for it.

definition:	first language translation:
sample sentence:	synonyms:

Organize the cards in review sets so you can practice them. Don't put words that are similar in spelling or meaning in the same review set as you may get them mixed up. Go through the cards and test yourself on the words or expressions. You can also practice with a partner.

VOCABULARY INDEX

Word	Page	CEFR† Level	Word	Page	CEFR† Level
accessible*	14	B2	lack	54	B2
affordable	14	C1	lead to	54	B2
anxiety	54	B1	make sense	44	off list
assess*	4	B2	mechanism*	34	C1
associate	24	C1	model	4	C2
awkward	54	B2	modify*	34	C1
charity	14	B1	muscle	35	B2
concept*	14	B2	nerve	35	C1
confirm*	44	B2	outcome*	14	C1
consistent*	24	C2	outgoing	54	C1
conventional*	4	B2	personality	44	B2
cooperate*	4	B2	poverty	4	B2
corporation*	14	B2	profits	4	B2
corresponding*	35	B2	radical*	34	C1
crucial	24	B2	react*	44	B2
demonstrate*	14	B2	remedy	24	B2
differ	54	B1	response*	14	B2
diverse*	4	B2	restore*	24	B2
donate	14	B2	result (n)	44	B2
effective	4	B2	severe	35	B2
empirical	24	C2	symptom	24	B2
entrepreneur	4	off list	synthetic	24	off list
expression	44	B2	tendency	44	C1
extrovert	54	C1	thrive	54	C1
fundamental*	14	C2	transmit*	35	C1
generate*	4	B2	trigger*	44	C1
inhibit*	24	off list	undergo*	34	C1
instinctively	44	C2	universal	44	B1
internal*	34	B2	upset	54	B1
introvert	54	C2	variable*	24	C1

†The Common European Framework of Reference for Languages (CEFR) is an international standard for describing language proficiency.

*These words are on the Academic Word List (AWL). The AWL is a list of the 570 highest-frequency academic word families that regularly appear in academic texts. The AWL was compiled by researcher Averil Coxhead based on her analysis of a 3.5-million-word corpus (Coxhead, 2000).

NOTES

NOTES

NOTES

NOTES